Andrea's Voice describes the pain of this illness more poignantly and accurately than any other writing on this subject. Thanks to Doris Smeltzer's courageous examination of her daughter's illness and death, Andrea may empower many others struggling with eating disorders to live.

—Margo Maine, PhD, psychologist and author of *Father Hunger*

Doris Smeltzer loved her daughter and left no stone unturned in caring for her. Her courageous and indomitable spirit and her capacity to tell a compelling story keep Andrea alive in readers' hearts and minds.

—Abigail Natenshon, MA, LCSW, GCFP, author of *When Your Child Has an Eating Disorder*

Andrea's Voice is the compelling story of one family's coping with the tragedy of bulimia. Not easy to put down, this is the deeply personal story of Smeltzer's journey through shock and grief. Andrea's own voice comes through poignantly, hopefully, in her poetry and journal entries.

—Frances M. Berg, MS, author of *Underage and Overweight*

I have such respect for your honesty and heart, and for Andrea's. Your book will be a light for many young women and their families.

—Annie Lamott, celebrated author and activist

This heartbreaking yet deeply impactful story will move readers to initiate change about how eating disorders are viewed in our country.

—Emme, supermodel and women's issues activist

Andrea's Voice tells the story of the tragic potentials of eating disorders through two powerful voices—Andrea, the daughter, and Doris, the mother. The end result is a deep understanding of the complexities of eating disorders and new compassion for those who suffer with them.

—Carole Normandi, MS, MFCC, and Laurelee Roark, MA, CCHT, coauthors of *It's Not About Food* and *Over It*

This book tells it all, told by a mother who has been there herself and who has dedicated her life to alerting others of the dangers of eating disorders. If you have a teenaged daughter, you especially need to read this book. If you're female and a teenager, this book could save your life.

—Hal Z. Bennett, author of *Write From the Heart*

Andrea's voice, as we hear it through her journal entries and poetry, resonates vibrantly within this heartbreaking, beautifully-written memoir of her mother's grief. Her life and premature death are emblematic of the enormous tragedies wrought by eating disorders.

—Kate Dillon, former supermodel, current plus size model

Andrea's Voice
Silenced by Bulimia

Her Story and Her Mother's Journey
Through Grief Toward Understanding

Doris Smeltzer
with Andrea Lynn Smeltzer
Foreword by Carolyn Costin, MA, MFT

gürze books

Andrea's Voice...Silenced by Bulimia

Her Story and Her Mother's Journey Through Grief Toward Understanding

© 2006 by Doris Smeltzer with Andrea Lynn Smeltzer

Gürze Books
P.O. Box 2238
Carlsbad, CA 92018
800-756-7533
www.gurze.com

Cover design by Johnson Design
Cover photo © Getty Images

Library of Congress Cataloging-in-Publication Data

Smeltzer, Doris, 1952-
Andrea's voice--silenced by bulimia : her story and her mother's journey through grief toward understanding / Doris Smeltzer with Andrea Lynn Smeltzer ; foreword by Carolyn Costin.
  p. cm.
Includes bibliographical references.
ISBN-13: 978-0-936077-01-7
ISBN-10: 0-936077-01-8
1. Smeltzer, Andrea Lynn, 1979-1999. 2. Smeltzer, Doris, 1952- 3. Bulimia--Patients--United States--Biography. 4. Bulimia--Patients--United States--Family relationships. I. Smeltzer, Andrea Lynn, 1979-1999. II. Costin, Carolyn. III. Title.
RC552.B84S54 2006
362.196'852630092--dc22

2006003642

Some names and identifying details of individuals have been changed to protect privacy. Permission has been granted for the use of names that have not been changed.

Andrea's journal entries, letters and poems are direct quotes—they have not been corrected for grammar. Every effort has been made to credit quotes Andrea may have used in her writing. Sadly, she did not always indicate when she was blending her thoughts with others' inspiring words. If we have neglected to credit others' words, please let us know and accept our apologies.

35790864

For Andrea Lynn Smeltzer
with much gratitude and forever love

Contents

Foreword

I have lived and breathed in the world of eating disorders for most of my life. Starting at the age of fifteen and lasting into my twentieth year, I suffered from anorexia nervosa. Now as I approach my fifty-second birthday, I am filled with the experience, knowledge and wisdom that twenty-eight years of treating eating disorder sufferers and their families has given me. I have seen the devastation and horror that an eating disorder wreaks on individuals and whole families. I have also witnessed the healing and soul growth that can occur.

Family members are often the unseen, untreated, unaccounted for victims in the eating disorder war. And, in the last five years, the number of books devoted specifically to family members or to professionals who educate and treat family members has increased significantly. I, along with three colleagues, did a review of eleven books of this nature in the July–September 2005 issue of *Eating Disorders: The Journal of Treatment and Prevention*. I was struck not only by the plethora of new information being published but also that the advice was tremendously varied, and in some cases, even contradictory.

One book said to monitor food intake and weigh your eating disordered child, while others said to leave this to professionals. Some books discussed not buying special foods while others suggested that if the person with the eating disorder would eat, then one should not fight over what foods she chose. There were suggestions for confronting purging behavior or locking up food, and there were suggestions that none of this would do any good. And there were several kinds of treatment options, but no real offers for what would work—for sure.

There are also many books written by family members who have experienced a son or daughter's eating disorder. In her book, *Eating With Your Anorexic*, Laura Collins wrote how she and her husband successfully treated her daughter at home following a new, promising but controversial, treatment known as the Maudsley Method. In *Slim To None*, Gordon Hendricks writes of his daughter's drawn-out, horrific and ultimately unsuccessful battle with an eating disorder and his anguish throughout. I have read so many of these books and seen so many television specials on eating disorders that I cringe at the thought of reading yet another. But no book has touched me as much as Doris Smeltzer's *Andrea's Voice*.

Andrea's Voice is not just another sordid tale or sobering look at the devastation of eating disorders. Through the reflections of Doris and the actual words of Andrea, taken from her letters, poetry and journals, the book reveals a tale of how good things can go so wrong—a tale which I believe may help save others. Parents will recognize themselves and their daughters in this story. Andrea should not have died, but her death and the subsequent writing of this book may very likely prevent others from suffering her fate.

Without blame or judgment, Doris seeks to find cause and responsibility to heal not just herself from the loss of her daughter, but society in general from the loss of something much greater. Bravely and honestly, Doris looks at her own contribution to the myriad of factors contributing to Andrea's bulimia, and in revealing this, will help others to do the same. Furthermore, she speaks to the contribution our current cultural climate plays in the development of eating disorders in a way that calls for introspection, growth and action. As Andrea's father and Doris's husband, Tom, says, "An eating disorder is a powerful teacher." Not only has Doris Smeltzer learned her lessons from this teacher, in writing *Andrea's Voice* she has gone on to become a powerful teacher herself.

—Carolyn Costin, MA, MFT
Director of the Monte Nido Treatment Center and
Founder of the Eating Disorder Center of California
Author of *The Eating Disorder Sourcebook* and
Your Dieting Daughter

Introduction

My daughter Andrea was not alone in her struggle with an eating disorder. "In the United States, as many as ten million females and one million males are fighting a life-and-death battle with...anorexia or bulimia. Approximately twenty-five million more are struggling with binge eating disorder."[1]

I wrote this book for those millions who deal with this illness every day, and for their loved ones and caregivers. Like the presentations my husband and I give on the subject of disordered eating, this book is a tribute to our daughter Andrea, who struggled with bulimia for a little over a year. Ultimately, that condition would take her life, but along the way were many powerful lessons that today help others heal.

Our family's experience taught me that a sufferer's loved ones and caregivers can hold the lifelines toward recovery. Each

---

1. National Eating Disorders Association (1-800-931-2237, *www.NationalEating-Disorders.org*) quoting Crowther et al., 1992; Fairburn et al., 1993; Gordon, 1990; Hoek, 1995; Shisslak et al., 1995.

of us must do our own internal work and discover what our relationship is to the disease. When all of us—Mom, Dad, siblings, friends and caregivers know these inner processes, we are much better able to be genuinely helpful and better able to cope with our own emotions throughout. I have chosen to share my inner processes, knowing that the most challenging part of this disease, for all involved, is internal.

What are the emotions with which the person with bulimia struggles? What are the feelings their loved ones face? There is no way to heal except through recognizing and dealing with all of these emotions. And there is no way to do that except by allowing ourselves to be vulnerable and open. So when it came to writing this book, that is what I was determined to do. In the pages that follow, I share my and our daughter's journey into the mysteries of both the disease and our internal workings, hoping that these inward glances may allow readers to peer carefully within themselves as well.

In the tenuous dance of life, we are all "fragile flames."[2] I first heard this descriptive expression in a song on one of the CDs that Andrea listened to frequently. My daughter knew that for a spark to glow brighter and stronger, the oxygen of honest self-exploration was necessary. May this book help your flame burn more brightly.

---

2. "Fragile flames": Jewel, "Innocence Maintained," Spirit, (New York, NY: Atlantic Recording Corporation, 1998), A82950-2, audio compact disc.

1.

This Lightness of Being

The joy is in the journey. [3]

−Anonymous

"You must give me five minutes, Officer, to tell my wife what you have just told me." My husband's measured words continued, "I will then call you back to answer your questions." My right hand tightened on Tom's strong shoulder. I stood to the left of his high-backed desk chair. I could not see his face, but my heart knew what he was about to tell me. He replaced the receiver in its cradle and swiveled the chair gently toward me. The room was filled with my husband's broad six-foot frame as he rose to face me, tears streaming into his closely cropped salt-and-pepper beard. His voice cracked with emotion as he relayed the message that I knew was coming and yet, for the previous tortured eight hours had prayed would not be true.

---

3. The quotes at the beginning of each chapter come from Andrea's journal of favorite quotations, which she began collecting, illustrating and recording at the age of thirteen.

"They've found the dead body of a young girl in the home where Andrea was house sitting."

My knees gave out, and a wail that sounded eerily familiar to my ears escaped my throat. Tom's swift arms caught me before I hit the floor. I continued downward with purpose. I had to be on the ground; I had to make my body small. In doing so, maybe I could disappear and this reality would not be able to find me. I wanted to evaporate into the ether. I sobbed in a small bundle on the floor of the study.

My senses came crashing back into the room when I heard Tom's voice, like a thunderbolt, yelling, "NO! God, please, NO!" The room shuddered as his bent body fell hard into the chair and his fist came down with shocking force on the desktop. I was amazed its glass surface did not splinter into broken shards, and disappointed, in an obscure, detached sort of way, that it had not. It would have been such a fittingly-tangible representation of that moment.

With effort, Tom straightened his body. "Doris, we must call back." Through his tears he continued, "The police officers and coroner need to question us. Until proven otherwise, they are treating this as a murder investigation."

I felt frozen in an alternate universe. How could they think that we could speak at that moment? Too numb, too frightened to argue, I acquiesced. Tom returned the call.

 *Andrea, 13, journal entry, October 25, 1993:*

I'll be 14 on Friday and I have a wonderful life ahead of me. Sometimes, like now, I just want to stop time and preserve the wonderful feelings. Someday, when I'm an adult, I'll be busy and stressed and I know I'll be able to look back and when I do I want to remember all the wonderful days when at some moment I just felt wonderful and happy and that no matter what disaster tomorrow has there's that wonderful feeling I can't explain that I can hold onto and remember. I have a wonderful life and an even better one ahead of me. *"Goals do far more for our world and for our character than gifts have ever done. So, go for your dreams, dear reader and let me know what happens."* That was in a newspaper. It was the advice the writer had for the person. I love that and I believe it with all my heart. My dreams are slowly starting to come true. I love taking that clipping out and reading it—so go for your dreams, dear reader, and let me know what happens...

I pulled myself off the floor and onto the nearby footstool. While Tom punched in the numbers, I wrapped my arms around my chest in a futile attempt to ward off the chill in the room. It was 3:30 in the morning and the summer shirt and shorts I had worn all day provided no protection from the cold. My teeth began to chatter and I realized that the chill was actually emanating from within me. I wanted desperately to run to the bathroom and vomit—my body responding naturally to the shock—but I could not allow myself to engage in the very act that may have helped kill my daughter. The thought was more gut wrenching than the nausea…I felt that to give in to this automatic response would somehow dishonor her. I could not allow that to happen. My head pounded as I braced myself for what was to come.

Tom was speaking to an officer. I heard his voice resonate as if through a thick curtain and surmised the questions from his careful responses. "Yes, sir. We were at our friends Jim and Karen's celebrating Father's Day. We last spoke to Andrea on Tuesday, five days ago. She said she'd call again the next day on my birthday, and if she missed us, then for sure on Father's Day. When we didn't hear, we knew something was wrong." Tom inhaled deep breaths while he listened. I could see the effort it took for him to respond, and yet his voice remained remarkably even. "Yes, that's right, she was there house sitting for Jana's parents, the Milhons. Andrea is a Resident Assistant at college and Jana is her Dorm Advisor." There was another long pause, and then Tom's steady voice. "Yes. We called the police earlier today, but when they would not enter the house we called and insisted that Jana go over and check on Andrea." In my body I felt a resurgence of the panicked frustrations I had endured during the previous five days.

Tom and I sat on the small, comfortably-cushioned sofa in Jim and Karen's living room after a late Father's Day dinner. Tom argued quietly with me about making a call to the police. Karen walked into the room as Tom again suggested that I was overreacting.

"Overreacting to what?" Karen tilted her head. One of her raised eyebrows touched the shock of short silver hair brushed to one side of her forehead.

Jim returned from the kitchen as I explained the situation. Placing his cardigan sweater across the back of the nearly identically colored brown sofa, he smoothed his receding hairline and agreed, "There's no way, buddy, that Andrea would miss your birthday and then Father's Day." Jim stood in front of us, his round lenses reflecting the light from the nearby hanging lamp. "Doris is right. You gotta check it out."

This support was exactly what I needed to persuade Tom to do as I had begged over the last few days. "See, Tom. I am not imagining things...there's something wrong. Now will you call the police?"

"We promised to give her space," Tom reminded. "She'll call when she's ready. If you're so sure there's something wrong, *you* call the police."

Leaning forward, I persisted doggedly, "If I call I'll just be seen as a hysterical mother and they'll do nothing. I know they'll listen to a man, especially a father, and take immediate action." I pleaded, "Please, Tom, if I thought I'd be effective I'd call, but I know they'll just blow me off. Please make the call."

Jim and Karen's concerned agreement with me convinced Tom to contact the police. They recorded the address and promised to get right back to us after they visited the place where Andrea was house sitting. We waited for nearly two hours until I could take it no longer and demanded that Tom call again.

When he hung up he reported, "They apologized for not calling back, but everything's fine."

I remember the relief I felt and how I shouted gleefully, "They saw her? They talked to Andrea?"

Tom acknowledged, "Not exactly, but they went out to the house. Things looked fine. Andrea's car is parked in the carport around back. She didn't answer their knocks, but they left a note on the door asking that she call her parents immediately."

I had difficulty containing myself. "They didn't go in the house?" I exclaimed, incredulous. "No. Tom, this is not okay. Somebody has to go into that house to see if she's there."

Tom repeated the explanation the police had given him. "They said that because there is no indication of foul play, it is not possible for them to enter the home, Doris. She's okay. She'll call."

I was no longer in denial. I finally allowed the fear that hovered just beneath my mind's radar to surface. I would not be deterred. "Somebody has to go into that house, Tom. There's no way Andrea would not have called on your birthday, and then to miss Father's Day…" My head shook with determination. "That's just not something Andrea would do. We have to get someone into that house. We must call Jana. She would have a key."

At that point, it was after midnight. We were still at Jim and Karen's place, an hour away from our home in Napa, California, and we could not remember Jana's last name. I insisted that Tom continue to do the calling. I knew that I would burst into tears if someone dared to resist my requests. Tom called the college's twenty-four-hour information line and miraculously got a human being. He summarized our situation. Fortunately, Jana and her husband lived on campus and the young man transferred the call.

Groggy with sleep, Jana declared, "She's gonna be sooo pissed when I wake her up."

"I know. I've told her mother the same thing."

I shouted from the background, "She'll get over it!" Jana later confirmed that the fact that Andrea's father called rather than me had immediately convinced her she needed to drag her husband out of bed and drive to her parents' home at that early hour of the morning.

Jana swore that she would take her cell phone and call us as soon as she entered the home. She told us that it was about a fifteen-minute drive, and that we could expect a return call in twenty minutes.

The call never came.

When Jana and her husband, Victor, arrived at her parents' home it appeared quiet and peaceful. Jana banged on her childhood bedroom window where she knew Andrea slept, hoping to rouse her before unceremoniously barging in on her. After a few knocks on the entry door went unanswered, Jana pulled out her key and turned the lock. The door had cracked but a few inches when the sickening and unmistakable smell of death hit her nose. Jana's heart sank as she closed the door without entering. Immediately she called the police. Within minutes the silent squad cars pulled into her parents' cul-de-sac. Jana watched in disbelief as her family's home became a crime scene, with she and Victor prime suspects in the death of the young woman inside. Jana was not permitted to make additional calls.

After thirty minutes of waiting for Jana's return call, my brain refused to believe the reassuring words Tom and I repeated over and over again. The fear that Andrea had been hurt or kidnapped or murdered prompted horrendous images to flash into my mind again and again. I could not allow these notions to sit in my brain for long, so I forced my mind to go into remote, to think of nothing. Yet I knew that the first twenty-four hours of an abduction were the most crucial. Why had we hesitated so long to take action? Seeking diversion, I grabbed a catalog from the end table and flipped the pages, not seeing anything, still trying to force my brain to numb, to stop thinking.

When two hours had passed with no word from Jana and no response to the countless messages we had left her, I looked at Tom and said, "I can't wait here any longer. I need to be in my own home." We left one final message on Jana's machine, letting her know that we had headed for home. We would be there in an hour and she should call us at that number.

The drive lasted an eternity. Neither Tom nor I spoke. The silence was punctuated only by the inexplicable sighs that escaped occasionally from deep within my chest. As soon as we pulled into the driveway we bolted from the car. We walked straight through the pitch-black living room to our study. The blinking of the message light was the only illumination in the small room. Tom sat at the desk and pressed the button. "This is Officer Bradley from the La Verne Police Department. Please call me at..." Tom jotted down the numbers and immediately returned the call.

A change in Tom's voice pulled me from my trance. His second call to the police had stretched into an eternity of answers to questions neither of us wanted to hear. My body was now shaking with uncontrollable spasms. My jaw clamped tightly as I attempted to control the clatter of my teeth. Officer Bradley asked to speak to me. All the questions seemed the same. "When was the last time you spoke to your daughter? Why is she here in this house? The woman who found her told us she was bulimic. Did you know that?" And then quietly, almost conspiratorially, "I have children of my own. What happened? Why would your daughter do this to herself?"

 Andrea Smeltzer, 19, six months before her death: [4]

My body moves rhythmically,
A lover's motion,
Sweet acid tickling the back of my throat
I come to my own rescue
and purge myself of evils, vice and sins.
I caress myself in a place no one else can reach...

My religion, my lover, my therapy
I am silent, reveling in my secret
the only time that tears occur by physical reflex,
not from pain or joy—just there
How beautiful that no one knows
The feeling of the soft, secret flesh
dark and warm and wet
Filling my hand with the decomposition from within
removing it, holding it, holding me

The rational, helpful purpose this serves for me
in painful discord with the consequences I am told of,
but have not yet felt.

---

4. Throughout this book, Andrea's selected journal entries are in chronological order. However, her poems are not presented chronologically.

The lightness of being when I know it is no longer in me
opposing the dark shame, the pounding pressure
behind my eyes...

Back on the safe side of the line,
betting on a supposed ability to stay there;
a dangerous game, a breaking of promises,
a denial of truth...

The seductive hand, whispering, aching
making up for, for everything, for you.
Let me pretend I belong to a different truth.
Let me have this that is wholly mine
For how long?

For how long this time can I run with the demon
and call her my friend?

It was dumbfounding to be asked to explain to another parent, who also happened to be an officer investigating your daughter's death, why your daughter struggled with bulimia. I did not believe that even Andrea could have stated the "why." I labored to form coherent sentences as I continued to fight the urge to run to the bathroom to relieve the nagging nausea, and yet here was a man asking, "How do I avoid this outcome for my own children?" and "Why? Why would she do this to herself?"

I stifled a scream. I kept thinking, *If we knew the answers to these questions we would not be speaking to you right now!* I tried to think clearly. Summoning all of my strength, I forced my words through a clenched, shaky mouth, amazed that sounds came out. "We've been...seeing...a therapist...she's guessed...at the cause...We...really...don't know."

I spoke in short gasps, attempting to gulp oxygen between phrases and verbalize between shivers. "Maybe…it was…worry over us…Andrea was…only eleven…when Tom and I…got sick." I swallowed hard and forced myself to go on, "I had cancer…Tom has…heart trouble. We really don't know…we've been learning…all we can, but…maybe fear…of our deaths contributed…how I wish we knew."

I wanted desperately to believe that the cause of Andrea's illness was not anything we could have controlled, could have changed. Yes, fear of losing us had played a part in Andrea's struggles. But there were several other contributing factors, we would find out later, many of them cultural and some directly related to who we were as people and as parents.

 Andrea, 13, during a vigil over my hospital bed after my third surgery for cancer, November 1993:

You cannot hear me
Though I wish more than anything you could
What will happen if you don't wake up?
How will the world keep going?
You can't leave me now
That's a selfish thought I know
But I've never lived without you
Never been away from you for more than a month
So how can I be expected to get through
eternity without you?

These are questions you can't answer I know
But I can't stop the surging feeling of emptiness inside
My world is falling apart and with it my mask

It is harder to smile now
Nothing makes me laugh anymore

Remember when you saved me
from monsters under the bed?
Who will save me from the monsters I face now?
I wished for a while that I never knew you
That your grave would mean nothing to me
But that hurt more than the pain of watching
your monotonous sleep

I pray that you're not in too much pain
Please come back home soon
The friends I didn't have,
the grandmother who wasn't there
The loving mother—you've been all of these to me
Sleep well...

Officer Bradley inquired if the coroner could speak to me.
As soon as he came on the line, I blurted out my first complete
sentence: "Did my daughter kill herself?" In that instant my mind
had flashed on one of Andrea's comments during our last conversation. Had she insisted I not make commitments for her because
she planned on taking her life that night? I had to know.

"No. No. Absolutely not." He confirmed with gentle care.
"I'm not yet sure what caused her death, but she did not com-
mit suicide."

Fresh tears flowed, "What happened? Can you make a
guess?"

"Mrs. Smeltzer, I would be doing just that, guessing. There
is the appearance of dried brown matter around her lips and

chin. This is just conjecture, but it may be that she choked on something she ate or maybe her own vomit, especially if she regurgitated while sleeping."

The guilt hit swift and sure. I gasped small in-and-out sobs. Why had I not thought to warn her to sleep with her head propped? She had suffered from reflux for weeks—a condition where gastric juices or small amounts of food from the stomach flow back into the esophagus and mouth. How could I not have alerted her to that danger?

The coroner's voice was very kind. He spoke slowly and respectfully of our daughter's body. I pictured Andrea's mass of short red curls encircling her oval face with its soft cheekbones and chiseled chin—a genetic gift from her father. As I tried to imagine dried brown matter near her mouth, my mind suddenly jolted with the realization that this was not the face the investigators were viewing. I shook my head violently to dislodge the horror of the image of five days of decay when the coroner confirmed my mind's knowing.

"I need to tell you...I am so sorry...but there is no possibility that you can have an open casket service, if that is what you were hoping for. The body is far too decomposed."

His words hung in the air like the stinging tendrils of a deadly jellyfish, even though I already knew that Andrea's body would be cremated—it was what she had instructed just a few weeks before.

Jocelyn, our then twenty-five-year-old daughter, had come home for a family dinner the night before Andrea was to leave for Southern California. I had played with Moe, Jocelyn's white boxer, while the four of us sat chatting after the meal. Unexpectedly I heard myself ask my daughters a question that had never occurred to me before. "You know, I just realized that you both know what to do if Daddy or I should die, but we have no idea what you would desire if, heaven forbid, something should ever happen to either of you." Wanting to ward off any negative energy these spoken words might have mysteriously invoked, my tight fist knocked on the wood of the dining table.

This question was motivated from the experience of having helped arrange, just two weeks prior, my mother's funeral. Throughout that ordeal I had experienced the frustration of not knowing my mother's wishes. I had found myself wondering over and over again, *What would she have wanted?*

Andrea wisecracked with her wry sense of humor, "I definitely want a professional mourner—one with cowboy hat, chaps and spurs."

I had forgotten about the stranger she and I had noticed sitting quietly in the back of the chapel throughout my mother's service. Afterward, as we gathered our things from the funeral home, I had asked my brothers and sisters if they knew the man with the cowboy hat. An employee happening by had offered, "Oh, he comes to them all. He's our local mourner."

At the table, Andrea and Jocelyn lapsed into a very funny, albeit macabre, routine about cemetery groupies, until I brought them back to my need for an answer.

"Seriously, I really want to know. What would you like us to do?"

Andrea instructed without hesitation, "Donate all my organs. Cremate whatever's left. And don't let anybody talk you into some fancy procedure or expensive urn or anything like that. I want the cheapest cremation possible!"

Knowing that Andrea wanted cremation did not diminish the sting of the coroner's words that echoed over the telephone line. Once again, the air abandoned my lungs. It had not occurred to me that I would be robbed of a final good-bye. "I won't be able...to see my daughter's body? I can't hold her...one last time?"

"I am so sorry. No. You don't want to see her body this way. It is unrecognizable. I am so very sorry."

The heavy weight that had become my heart dropped deeper into my chest. I overheard Officer Bradley say that he needed to speak with me again. The coroner quickly imparted his condolences once more and handed the phone back to the officer, who made a few more queries. His voice was empathic, and yet his need for explanation overrode the agony he must have known his questions caused. I sensed he could not help himself when I heard his final question, "Looking at the picture on your daughter's driver's license, I see that she was beautiful, and didn't look overweight. Is that correct?"

I was initially stunned, and then remembered our own ignorance at the start of Andrea's illness just thirteen months before. Tom and I had come to understand at least this much: Eating disorders are NOT about food or weight. Because they often begin with that focus, many people erroneously assume that is how they continue. These illnesses quickly become coping mechanisms, a way to numb, to avoid overwhelming feelings and acquire a sense of control. I actually felt torn by my desire to educate this person and my need to get off the phone to call Jocelyn... I felt I must hold my one remaining daughter. My answer to the officer was choked out through sobs. "She...was...perfect. No, she was not overweight...she was beautiful...in every way."[5]

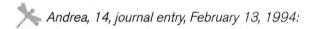 *Andrea, 14, journal entry, February 13, 1994:*

I have realized that I have truly incredible parents. I get very mad at them sometimes but when push comes to shove they are very cool! Today I had lunch with Ken and Kylie at La Crepe Café and then went to a movie (*My Father, The Hero*). Kylie was definitely stoned. Tonight when I told my parents, they were great. They don't mind that she's my friend and she smokes pot. They want me to make good choices but they know they can't shield me from life—it's out there—What is cool is that they see me as a real person making decisions leading me into adulthood....

This was an incredible weekend. Jocie [Andrea's sister] took me to see *My Fair Lady*. It was hilarious! Then we had a great slumber party. I saw *Phantom of the Opera*. It was incredible! It was erotic and sensual and spectacular! I'm going to be on that stage someday!

---

5. Today, I do not use the term "overweight." Its use is discomforting to me. It mistakenly implies that there is an appropriate weight that has been exceeded.

Andrea had been making herself vomit for thirteen months, an extremely short time in the context of most such disorders. She was in therapy; we all were. The experts had assured us that she would be fine; she would heal. What had gone wrong? Had we failed as parents? What had happened? In those wee hours of that morning in June 1999, we were only guessing. We did not have a clue.

2.

Magical Notions of Birth

You must do the thing you think you cannot do.

—Eleanor Roosevelt

During the first few years after Andrea's passing I lived life through a series of flashbacks. They were often unpleasant and came by the dozens each day. How else could I determine where I had gone wrong? Andrea was no longer here to inform me. However, when she had been, she had assured me, "This is not your fault, Mom. This illness is mine." Comforting words that Andrea knew I needed to hear. Yes, the illness was hers. But was I its cause? I have awakened to the lies that I told myself as a parent, lies that in many ways form the foundation of our culture—lies that were difficult for me to recognize without the neck-wrenching jolt of Andrea's death, which forced my eyes to see in a new way. I had not caused Andrea's eating disorder, but I had contributed to how she felt about her self and her body through the ways I felt about my self and my body.

My unbidden recollections revealed the negative behaviors I had modeled for our daughters. The countless times I insulted my body in front of them, refused to wear bathing suits due to a "fat stomach," and my need to wear large, oversized clothing in which to hide my body. At five feet seven inches I had always hovered on one side or the other of a size twelve, a number considered gigantic by today's unrealistic, media-driven, skeletal standards, but still I embarked on numerous diets. I gained and lost the same twenty pounds over and over again. I counted calories and wondered aloud how much fat each food item contained. I read food labels incessantly, and had burdened my body with various on-again, off-again exercise regimens.

After I had become an educator, on many an evening my daughters listened to me lament about how I was a lousy teacher, while I blithely disregarded much evidence and testimony to the contrary. Daily, I put on display for our daughters my intense body dissatisfaction, dieting and perpetual lack of self-confidence. Did I think they could not hear? Did I believe they would not see? How did I think Jocelyn and Andrea could feel *good enough* about themselves when I did not feel that about myself? The lessons I learned so well at my mother's knee I unintentionally imparted to my daughters, twenty-four hours a day, seven days a week during the formative years of their lives.

Beyond the behaviors I modeled, when I return to our daughters' beginnings, their births, it was Jocelyn's that I assumed was dramatically flawed, not Andrea's. I had given birth to Jocelyn "out-of-wedlock" back in the early seventies when unwed motherhood was far more stigmatized than today. I gave birth to Andrea "legitimately" four years after Tom and I got back together and married.

Jocelyn's conventional hospital birth serves as a textbook study in the doctor-controlled birthing practices common at the time. I recall how the obstetrician whisked into the delivery room shortly after I received a numbing epidural.

"Where in the hell is her goddamned husband?" he demanded of the delivery room with anger.

I pulled my head up from the uncomfortable, horizontal gurney and began, "Doctor, remember, I'm not marri—"

The doctor immediately caught his error and, with a kinder tone, interrupted. "Oh, it's you. I'm sorry. I forgot." With that he gave me a large episiotomy, cutting from the bottom of the vagina to what later felt like the small of my back, and ordered the nurse to push. I felt stunned when the nurse put both her hands at the top of my belly's roundness and pushed with all her might. From that moment on, anesthetized from the waist down, I became no more than an observer of a very bizarre play. It hurt to know that if I had a husband at my side the physician would have permitted him to coach me to push with each contraction, allowing my baby to leave the womb gradually. This doctor showed no such patience with a young unwed mother. He could get on with his day within five minutes by demanding that my child be expelled in one uterine cramp through the hefty thrust of an obliging nurse.

Jocelyn's birth sits in diametrical opposition to the experience Tom and I arranged for Andrea's arrival. I swore that her delivery would be different. I would become informed, learn everything I could about how to compassionately welcome a child into the world. There would be no hospital involved this time. Love and the warmth and comfort of our own home would embrace our baby, with Tom and Jocelyn playing active roles. I truly believed that I had to undo the errors I had made with Jocelyn's first days, that a bonding birth experience at home could guarantee our resiliency as a family and increase our abilities to weather misfortune. The actual event went so beautifully that it reinforced these magical notions of birth.

 Andrea, 18, watching Tom in his hospital bed before open-heart surgery, July 1998:

I know where I got my chin
angular and strong
the outline still there on this man
this man on the bed, sleeping.
He gave me this chin.

    It is something we share
    a tie that even we cannot break
    the startling proof in photographic evidence.
    It would seem that he should
    show up square and I round
    or I should be a desert and he the ocean.
    But we are not.

One eye squints closed when I smile
it is clear that this too is his legacy
Perhaps the only common ground we have ever shared
So important now that there *is* something we share.

Is this then what binds us together?
Empirical evidence of love
proving to the world and myself
that I am my Father's daughter.

I love this chin, his chin
it never argues, or annoys, or angers
it holds character and smiles and pain
it is so easy to love this chin.

Sometimes it seems
these features are our only commonality
Sometimes I wonder
if any of his other stuff made it inside me
But I watch him listen,
hear the news he doesn't want to hear
And I see him take a breath and then another
And I am so proud to have my father's chin.

Labor with Andrea began at around four o'clock in the morning. I remember sitting for a while in a hot tub of water, attempting to time my contractions when I heard an odd, forlorn animal-like cry filling the night air outside our Southern California home. The unknown yowl resounded through the open bathroom window. I had never heard such a sound before. I left the bath and stood with a towel wrapped around my body, listening to the reverberations of this intensely sad cry. My uterus cramped strongly with the next pain. Because six-year-old Jocelyn slept in the adjoining room, I resisted the temptation to add my voice to the heart-wrenching wail coming from outside. Instead I breathed deeply through the contraction while holding on to the windowsill and leaned my swollen belly against the wall of the tiny room. I never discovered the source of this sound and did not, at the time, feel a connection between its occurrence and our daughter's birth.

No longer able to accurately time the erratic comings and goings of my cramping, the bathroom contraction convinced me that I needed to awaken Tom. He called the nurse midwife thirty minutes later to tell her he was still checking me for false labor, but wanted to give her a "heads-up" just in case it was the real thing.

I shouted over his voice, "Trust me, it's real!" Tom had obviously paid great attention to the "false labor" lessons taught in our many childbirth classes. Although my dagger-like glance as he hung up the phone told him, "Enough with the false labor thing," I basked in the support and encouragement I felt at having my husband at my side. Awakened by our voices, Jocelyn ran into the living room to play the part that she, too, had rehearsed over the past six months.

Once Tom realized my pains were bona fide, our efforts became synchronized: Tom coaching, Jocelyn offering words of encouragement, patting my brow with a wet washcloth, and me breathing toward birth. An hour after calling the nurse midwife, as Tom helped me roll back from an uncomfortable side position, my water broke. I grabbed his shoulder. My jaw snapped shut in an attempt to resist the urge to push. Out of gripped teeth I hissed, "Tom, look, see…I think the baby's coming." I continued my shallow breathing, completely unaware of the acute pain caused by my vise-like grasp on his shoulder.

Tom's apparent hesitation exasperated me until he bravely squeaked out, "If you'll let go, I can check." At that moment I heard the midwife's car door slam in the driveway.

With immense relief, I released my stronghold on my husband while Jocelyn opened the front door and yelled, "My mom wants to push, but my dad's makin' her blow."

With Jocelyn's shouted warning, the nurse midwife knew to grab her bag before entering our living room. She went immediately to the kitchen to call for her assistant and to scrub up. After a quick check on my progress she announced cheerily, "Feel free to push any time now, Doris."

What a difference from before…able to assume whatever position I chose, no predelivery enema, no uncomfortable shaving of the vaginal area, no episiotomy, no epidural, no nurse bearing down on my abdomen…pushing provided a release topped only by the conviction that *this* time I was doing it right.

 Andrea, 18, observing our relationship during Tom's open-heart surgery, July 1998:

She is his advocate
Sometimes silent, sometimes screaming
Always watching

They are two halves
coming together from different wholes
not quite a perfect match
fitting together anyway, somehow

Like oil and vinegar
When they are shaken no lines of separation are visible

and then they begin to separate again
At the last minute they hold on and don't let go.

> They are not fluent in each other's languages
> But like a stubborn tourist,
> they persist and settle in
> Almost a native but sometimes still
> so foreign and strange.
> —How could you?
> —I don't know.

He is her sounding board
Sometimes critical, sometimes supporting
Always trying

> It is inconceivable that they are partners
> and yet it is so right!
> A fish and a bird are lovers
> and I know where they make their home.

As the sun rose, splashing rays of warmth through the picture window, I gave birth to our second child. Tom gently laid the squirming new life on my belly while we waited for the blood to stop coursing through the umbilical cord. As I rubbed the white coating of vernix into the little body, I glanced down and saw what our preoccupation had prevented us from noticing, "Oh,…we have a girl!" The perfect shape of her head startled me, her face like that of a porcelain doll with no hint of the trauma of birthing.

Jocelyn reminded Tom, "Daddy, we need to bond with her, skin-to-skin." Jocelyn removed her pajama top and waited for her turn to hold her new sister tight against her bare chest, assuring the deep and abiding friendship that would develop between them during Andrea's last years here. Tom took Andrea back into his arms and pressed her close before returning her to my breast.

With this, our "perfect" birth, I made up for the many errors made with Jocelyn's. In my mind, our daughters were now inoculated forever against doubting their own worth or questioning whether or not they were loved. Andrea, unlike Jocelyn, was breastfed for two years, and when she was introduced to solids at six months (as recommended by the leading nutritionists) they were homemade from the freshest ingredients. An eating disorder in our home? NEVER!

3.

A Silver Flash of Dragonflies

Be glad you had the moment.

—Steve Shagan

Soon after Andrea's death, I found myself driving aimlessly through our hometown of Napa amidst pre-Christmas traffic. My brain, nearly always in flashback mode, ran down two tracks—one a reflection of the torturous six months that had passed since Andrea died, the other focused on an intense need to buy a Christmas gift for Andrea, even though she was no longer here. For the first time ever, there were no decorations, no tree, no carols sung in our home. Jocelyn, her husband Tracy, Tom and I planned to leave town for the holiday to hunker down together, away from family, friends, memories. We had agreed to exchange a few small items and had acquired new Christmas stockings for the occasion to avoid the painful task of pulling out the old, traditional socks.

The tears that had become as much a part of my countenance as my smile or frown streamed down my face as I conversed in the car out loud with the daughter I longed to hold again. "Annie, I know how silly this seems, but to not buy you a gift feels so wrong. Please guide me, Hon, to where I can buy something to honor you." I felt certain that I would know the gift when I saw it.

Andrea, 18, first stanza of a ten stanza poem [subsequent stanzas to follow] written as a Mother's Day gift, May 1998, one year before her death:

There is a love so strong it never leaves me.
I am five years old, being sung to sleep in a rocking chair
Your arms around me keeping me safe
So much love.

There is a patience so complete it never gives up on me
I am 12, angry and hurt, trying to smash your infusaport[6]
Eyes that look into mine as you pin my arms
"I love you but I hate what you're doing."
You hurt, but you stay strong and teach me to be human

I parked near downtown and walked toward our town square, buttressed by the day's brisk wind. The crisp cold jarred my mind back to its second track, the reflections on the first 180 days that I had somehow survived. There had been a strange paradoxical feeling of eternity and immediacy since June 16. That morning in Tom's study had happened a lifetime ago and yet the sharp, palpable pains I continued to experience made it feel like a mere moment had passed. Two memorial services had

6. infusaport: subcutaneous port surgically inserted in my chest through which chemotherapy and blood transfusions were injected.

been held to commemorate our daughter's life. The second service in September had been a heartfelt gift from Andrea's classmates and colleagues at her alma mater, Pitzer College, in Southern California. It was held after the return to campus of many friends who could not attend the first celebration of her life in June.

I thought of the surprise mass e-mail that had been sent out to university campuses across the nation from the Claremont College Health Director declaring "Andrea's Voice" a most powerful eating disorder presentation (although the informal chat we had with students after the memorial service was simple, and bore little resemblance to the talk we present today). In those early months my battered heart felt cocooned by the tremendous love, support, help and guidance from friends, family and colleagues, which allowed for the miraculous unfolding of my soul's work.

With wonder and gratitude, I recalled those who aided my abrupt transition from a second grade teacher to a job at the district level, those who helped with the design of our Andrea's Voice brochure and presentation to be given at the half dozen speaking engagements booked within days of the prophetic e-mail, and the volunteer efforts of a techno-savvy colleague and friend in getting our *AndreasVoice.org* website up and running. It was this outpouring of support that kept me upright and allowed me to rise and dress and function on a daily basis with all the appearance of a "normal" being.

> There is a confidence I draw on when I am in need
> I am 14 years old being told not to quit
> A voice that penetrates me,
> "You must do the thing you think you cannot do."

So, I go to Spain.
So much faith in me.

There is an understanding so deep when I am in turmoil
I am 16, hurt, hurt, hurt, turned down for prom.
A hand that holds mine, taking away the need
to explain my tears
You know. I am not alone.

All of these thoughts passed through my brain as I wandered by the shops on the plaza. There had been a rare moment of clarity when it felt as if my entire life had been an apprenticeship, a training for the work that continued to be revealed in slow, and yet purposeful steps. I stopped to contemplate this mystery, and happened to glance upward. The sign above my head read "Silver Sensations."

There is a friendship deeper than any I have known
I am 17 and we are off on an adventure
A laughter that blends with mine
as we swim in Palm Springs

We have so much fun together.

There is a bond that is unbreakable
I am 18, in college and calling home every day
I cannot wait to chat. Share and listen even when
I have nothing to say
You make me feel special.

I walked inside and I knew. I whispered, "This is it, isn't it Annie? This is where I'll find your gift." The shop looked newly opened. Its silver jewelry was arranged around a décor of stars, comets and moons. Dominating the store's center was a tiled, round well painted with planets. A giant blue fish hovered in mid-wiggle above the well, spewing a stream of water into the fountain's depths. The entry floor welcomed with a large, brightly painted orange and yellow smiling moon, reminiscent of the moon mirror that hung in Annie's bedroom. My heart lurched. "Oh, Annie, what fun we would've had looking through this store together." The thought brought the ever-waiting tears and I glanced away from the kind woman who offered to help, quietly responding, "I'm just looking, thank you."

Four weeks before Andrea's death, without knowing the agony that awaited, I felt emotionally knocked to my knees by my mother's passing due to Alzheimer's-induced pneumonia. The Catholic priest who spoke at length of faith and life after death moved us out to the cemetery after Mom's church service. Andrea and I walked together. I had felt her tensing during the priest's eulogy and could tell by the intent look on her face that she would share her thoughts with him. As we approached, she looked directly into his eyes and challenged, "Do you really believe all that you said today?"

Taken aback, the priest replied, "With all my heart. It is by these tenets that I live my life."

Andrea's face softened a bit. "It is how I wish to live my life as well." The two of them then engaged in a lively dialogue about living a spiritual life.

There is a confident, hopeful, and strong young woman.
She has become this way because of you.

The faith you placed in her is now her belief
that she will succeed
The Love you gave her
is now the inner safety net of self-esteem she falls on
And the laughter you share brings a smile to her face
on the worst days.
It is because of you that she has the courage to try,
The strength to stick with it,
And the hope of new adventures.

Father O'Connor, a stranger to our family prior to presiding at my mother's funeral, telephoned the day after we heard the news of Andrea's passing. My brother had told him of our tragedy and he felt compelled to call, not only with his condolences, but also with his desire to speak at our daughter's memorial service. After a number of conversations back and forth—we already had a minister for Andrea's service and were unsure of the protocol involved in adding another—the priest revealed to us the reason for his passionate need to speak at her service. He related how Andrea's query the few weeks before had touched him deeply. He disclosed, "In my forty-odd years of priesthood, no one has ever asked me that question. She bravely confronted my words with such seeking, such a burning desire to know. I feel an inexplicable connection to your daughter. "

At Andrea's memorial service, this regally-clad priest narrated a poignant story of the dragonfly's life cycle. It made a fine metaphor for life after death. He described how the dragonfly nymph begins its life under water. All of its sustenance, indeed all of its needs, are met in this fluid environment. It is surrounded by its brothers and sisters and feels nourished in the shadow world beneath the water's surface. He then told of the nymph's intense experience of transformation into an adult dragonfly with wings. How it enters a vast universe of beauty beyond its wildest imaginings, and although it can fly over its previous home and even see its brothers and sisters along the water's edge, it can never return. It must wait until they, too, enter the next cycle of their life to be united once more.

Early the morning after we returned home from the intense emotion of Andrea's Southern California memorial service, I stood looking out our bedroom window. My arms rested on the tall windowsill as I stared out at the lushly green-leafed apple and almond trees. My mind felt numb with emotion. I looked but did not really see. A silver-streaked flash, followed by another and then another, begged my eyes to focus. I forced my mind to take note. What was that? Suddenly, I realized that the area right outside our bedroom window had filled with small, darting dragonflies—hundreds of them. I looked with awed wonder. How could so many dragonflies appear in one place, especially with no nearby source of water? I woke Tom. We stood and stared at this small miracle. We have associated Andrea with dragonflies ever since.

> There is a tightrope we walk called life
> You put me on it when you gave birth to me
> For a long time you carried me, then you held
> my hand, and then you told me you believed in me.
> You never hovered so close that you overpowered
> me and caused me to fall

But the presence of your hand was always there
Even now
You balance me.

I love you,
Andrea

Gazing into the glass display cases of the jewelry store, I continued to search for a Christmas gift to honor Andrea. The crystalline dragonfly earrings were so small that my eyes missed them when I first glanced. I was pulled to look again, and I knew. As the woman arranged the red tissue paper around my treasure and stuffed it into the tiny black gift bag, she asked cheerily, "So, is your Christmas shopping complete?"

I remember answering, "Now it is."

In the early years after Andrea's death, the infinitesimal satisfaction garnered from honoring acts, such as buying small gifts, was always shortened by my need to replay, again and again, troubling events and conversations. These painful, inexhaustible loops of tape—apparently stuck on rewind and repeat—tortured me by illustrating more appropriate responses that were based solely on the wisdom of hindsight. One such well-reviewed conversation was during a phone call received from Andrea the year before her death. We were coming to the end of a sweet thirty-minute chat when I heard a catch in her voice. Andrea often needed a pleasant "preamble talk" while she mustered the courage to say what was really on her mind. I knew that I needed to ask for more or the fleeting opportunity to hear her deepest thoughts would pass. I queried, "Annie, what's wrong?"

With first a pause and then a quick intake of breath she divulged, "I made myself throw up last night, Mom."

An immediate, overwhelming sense of dread enveloped me. I had the instantaneous, seemingly irrational thought, I'm going to lose her to this! My knees gave out and I hit the floor. Relieved that my daughter could not see my body's instinctive response, I kept my voice steady and revealed, "Annie, this is way beyond my areas of expertise. I don't know anything about this. Are you willing to get help?"

She replied seriously, "Yes."

We would not discover until a few weeks before her passing that this response was not entirely true.

4.

To Still Be Me

What would life be if we had no courage to attempt anything?

–Vincent Van Gogh

"I wanna be a foreign exchange student!" Andrea tossed her gym bag down as she entered the front door. She had just been dropped off at home after her badminton class at the community college. Overflowing with fourteen-year-old exuberance she expounded, "I have it all figured out. Two of the girls in my P.E. class have just been accepted to Ivy League schools with full scholarships and everything. I asked them how they got in and they said they'd lived for a year in a foreign country. They're sure that made the difference in their college applications, because they're smart, but, you know, they weren't, like, the absolute top of their class." Without taking a breath Andrea sped on, "This is perfect. I'm rated only about tenth in my class,[7] there's no way I'll

---

7. Today, I am appalled that my daughter could quote this number so blithely. What is the message we give students when we publish, on every report card, their class ranking? What message did I give when I confused her rank with my abilities as a parent?

get the scholarships Jocelyn did and you can't afford to send me to the colleges I want. This is PERFECT! Whadayathink??"

 First letter home from Spain, September 10, 1994:

Dear Mom and Dad (and Jocie and Tarri if they read this),[8]
    Today I arrived in Cuenca. My host family met me at the bus station. I am sharing a room with Evita. She is 16. She is really sweet and I love her already. I think that she is very pretty also. My mother is also pretty and slender (in an adult woman with 5 kids sort of way) too! She is sooo nice! My brother Raul is basically ignoring me so far but he's also a 15-year-old guy so it's not strange. Sabina (14) is very pixyish (sp?) her hair is cut short and her ears point just slightly but I think she is very pretty. She is very young. I mean I can relate and talk better with Evita. My 2 younger brothers, Roberto, 13 and Diego, 11, think I'm "ok." That was said with multiple shrugs. Diego, Evita and Sabina speak just a little bit of English. My mother speaks only Spanish and I think my father does too.… Evita took me to a bar this afternoon. It is so weird to legally be allowed in there and legally be allowed to order alcohol. They had beers but I just had a coke. The bar was so cool. It had all this music playing and I kept meeting friends and family of Evita. I already knew about the cheek kissing greeting thing but knowing about it does not prepare you for when someone gets really close to you and does it.…

---

8. Tarri: Jocelyn's then best friend who lived with us the summer before Andrea left for Spain.

Food here is weird and I have a very small appetite as I miss you but I'm having fun. Hopefully, my appetite stays small. Well just remember, jeans and slippers pronto! And remember I love you. Stay safe and healthy and know that I am in good hands.

I love you all, Andrea

I loved it when Andrea was in one of her expansive, "anything in the world is possible" moods. They were a rare joy to behold, especially when contrasted with her dark, "back OFF!" personality swings. Almost in unison Tom and I echoed, "Well, that's certainly something to think about someday."

"No, you don't understand. I need to go next year, as a sophomore. I can't go during my junior year. That's the year that really counts on college applications and I don't want to miss my senior year. If I go *after* graduation, I won't be able to include it in my applications. I *have* to go my sophomore year."

 Letter home, Friday, September 30, 1994:

Hey guys—How are you? It was wonderful to talk to you yesterday! I love getting caught up on all the family news. Well I'm in Latin class right now. I know what you're thinking—"Why aren't you paying attention?" Well let me tell you the way school operates. The teacher doesn't care about you. They want to finish their job as quickly as possible—so they stand at the front of the classroom—lecture then give the homework assignment then leave! They stand up there and lecture and I don't understand a thing.... The only good part about school is English! And the new friends I'm making! I'm enclosing a class schedule so every day you will know the exact tortures I'm undergoing. And guess what? Today at break somebody told me that I was hard to understand because I have such a heavy accent! I DON'T HAVE AN ACCENT! EVERYONE AROUND ME HAS AN ACCENT!!!

...Evita and I get along really well. Evita is just a little misdirected in some areas. Like in telling her parents everything she should. They don't know she's repeating a year of school. They don't know she has a boyfriend and her mother does not know she smokes (her father does).

"Aren't you too young?" I stammered as I attempted to buy time to think. "I can't imagine that they allow students to go at such a young age." Although Andrea's strong will had not been a difficulty for Tom during her childhood, it had always been a challenge for me. Instead of seeing the majority of her many mood changes as a natural part of development and attempts at individuation, I often interpreted them personally, seeing them as challenges to my "parental authority." My misguided interpretations caused us to feel out of sync much of the time. Early on, Andrea was able to push my buttons in a way that often frightened me (unheeded indicators that *my* individuation needed work), but the idea of her leaving for a year hurt too much to even consider.

Andrea paused. Apparently, she had not thought of the age limit. "I don't know. I'll find out...but can I do it? Is it possible?" Tom and I exchanged glances. He encouraged, "Find out the costs and all the particulars, and we'll see."

Andrea did the research and came to us with her discoveries.

It was evident immediately that the costs of an exchange program were beyond our reach, but we hated to discourage her exuberance. We attempted to stall her...surely it would be wiser to wait for a year, maybe two. That would have the double benefit of allowing time for us to put some money aside for the experience and for her to meet the minimum age requirement of fifteen.

We tried to present all the realities that had not occurred to her—the pain of leaving her family for an entire year at fourteen, the fact that she did not speak a foreign language, the maturity she would gain that might make coming home to finish two years of high school difficult. She rebutted each concern with a well-thought-out argument.

We were not thoroughly convinced, but after much discussion finally agreed to a compromise. If she could figure out a way around the obstacles of finances and the age restriction she would have our unconditional support. We assumed that this would be a fine learning experience, that even if she could convince the intercultural group to waive their age requirement, there would be no way she could come up with the money. "Life" would say "No" to our daughter, not us.

 Journal entry, November 1994:

> I remember watching movies on rainy days in the living room. I remember the wood-burning stove with the pot of water with cinnamon making the house feel warm and smell good. I remember dancing in the living room with the lights off, talking to people in my head and making up fantastic stories.

I remember reading in my room, lying on the floor up against my bed. I remember listening to music and looking out my window. I remember taking my goats on walks around the neighborhood.... I remember Sunday mornings reading the paper and eating breakfast with my family. I remember cooking, especially with Jim and Karen. I remember the drive to their house and the dinner parties we always had. I remember playing under my tree in the front yard and the sweet smell of cut grass from mowed lawns.

I remember planning surprises for Mom and Dad with my sister and cleaning the house to soundtracks of musicals. I remember Thanksgiving—the huge, wonderful dinner and being warm and full and at peace and eating leftovers for weeks.

I remember Christmas, the routine, the surprises. Decorating the tree to Christmas carols, spending the day of the 25th in leisure examining our gifts—The church service.

I remember the little traditions, "We're in central Benicia, Daddy." I remember camping with Dad before I left [for Spain] and the bead store in Arcata and I remember going into the city with my father for my visa and I remember my last home meal—Lemon Broccoli Chicken.

And I remember the morning I left how hard it was to say goodbye.... And I remember how I always used to re-arrange my furniture, and leaving "Andrea Detritus" all over the place....

And I remember the times where everything was just perfect and I never wanted the day to end. And how good

it felt to cook for Jocelyn and taking her cookies at work. And I remember talking myself through hard situations and living in my own made-up world in my head. And I remember the weekend nights my parents would go out and I would get a T.V. dinner and a movie and stay up late all by myself pretending to be in the movie.
And I remember sometimes going out for breakfast with Jocelyn...and sometimes how Mom would decide just to go to a movie and we'd all go and have fun.... And I remember being happy and sad and lonely and at peace and growing up and changing so I could come here. I haven't left any of that behind. It's a part of me. It is what has made me me and it will always be warm and safe.... I remember love.

With gusto, Andrea embarked on her goal to study abroad. She arranged for an interview in our home with the program's local representatives, and modeled the maturity needed for them to agree to waive their age requirement. She applied for a scholarship and wrote countless letters requesting financial assistance from friends, family members and local businesses. In exchange for support, she promised letters throughout her adventure, allowing contributors to share in her experience.

Responses started coming in, and to our amazement Andrea generated the money she needed. Tom and I realized that we were unprepared for this possibility. We did not really believe it could happen. Now we were left to grapple with our own emotions and fears. As her mother, I was not ready to let Andrea go out into the world for an entire year at such a young age.

Journal entry written in class, November 15, 1994:

And so I made a very important decision last night. I paid almost $7,000 to come here to be a different person. That's a whole lot of money. So I'm going to stop sitting on my butt feeling sorry for myself because I don't fit in and do something about it! I don't know how but I do know that the power to change is entirely within me. I will not allow others to define my mood, or my mission.

At first I thought that if I did "as the Romans" I would become different overnight—fit in. All is perfect. But that doesn't work—I have to still be me. I can't get lost in the shuffle. I'm still the same person. Coming here just gave me the *opportunity* to be different. It didn't automatically change me. I have to do that part…"and it's hard and it hurts and it takes knowledge you don't have but will when you're finished…. And you learn that you really are brave, that you really are strong, that you really can survive."[9]

My daughter was motivated by more than just the need to look good on a college application and to learn a second language. She longed for the confidence and self-acceptance that the experience of living abroad would provide. She felt sure that this would be the answer to many of her insecurities. An unstated goal that is revealed through various journal entries was Andrea's need to get away, to run from a family, indeed a world, where she did not feel she fit. She was moody, not chipper like her sister. During her teen years, her father's sense of humor irritated her, and my desire for her to "just be happy" invalidated the strong

---

9. Author unknown.

emotions she did feel. She was not happy, and she was tired of pretending. If she left, she could become whomever she wanted. She could reinvent herself. She could come back to a changed world because she would be a changed person who no longer needed the masks she wore.

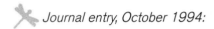 *Journal entry, October 1994:*

...I'm FINE. I'm just all mixed up inside. Suddenly right and wrong have switched poles and I don't know my own name. Is a name an identity? Does switching names allow you to assume a new identity or is it all in your mind and doesn't really matter? Am I just in dis-equilibrium again? Run out of schemas and too tired to make more?

What the hell is nuclear fusion anyway? It is not always comfortable being a mermaid. There is no place to stand.[10] In a parallel universe are our dreams their reality? Why is there no 's' at the end of the third person present simple verb? Can self-pity on a rainy day equal wet jeans for pure misery value any day of the week? Does all the shit we

---

10. Robert Fulghum, *All I Really Need To Know, I Learned in Kindergarten: Uncommon Thoughts on Common Things* (New York: Ivy Books, 1988), 82-83. A reference to this story: "She did not relate to being a Giant, a Wizard or a Dwarf. She knew her category. Mermaid. And was not about to leave the game and go over and stand against the wall where a loser would stand. She intended to participate, wherever Mermaids fit into the scheme of things. Without giving up dignity or identity. She took it for granted that there was a place for Mermaids and I would know just where. Well, where DO the mermaids stand? All the 'Mermaids'—all those who are different, who do not fit the norm and who do not accept the available boxes and pigeonholes? Answer that question and you can build a school, a nation, or a world on it.... It is not true, by the way, that mermaids do not exist. I know at least one personally. I have held her hand." 82-83.

get taught in school actually have meaning or would we be just as well off to chuck it all, go to the mountains and be at one with nature and peace? If the world as we know it were destroyed and people actually had to live out in nature would we be content with that or would the need to be bigger and better begin anew? Does age have relevance or can people interact together in the same ways regardless of age? This feels wrong. I'm very disoriented. Are guys truly ever of the same species? Happiness is being random.

Andrea and I attended the orientation night held at the University of California at Davis for prospective travel-abroad students. Adults who participated in the exchange experience many years ago and youth who had recently returned had the opportunity to tell of their experiences overseas. In addition to the ways that lives were changed by the adventure, the weight that the youth could expect to gain during their year in a foreign country became a repeated theme throughout the evening. Each person who spoke felt it important to note how he or she had gained from fifteen to forty pounds during their time away. With each utterance, Andrea glanced my way. After the third reference to weight she leaned sideways and whispered into my ear, "Great, as if I'm not already heavy enough."

During the previous few years, Andrea had begun gaining the weight that puberty requires of the female form. Sadly, I did not have the wisdom to celebrate this change and to assure her that weight gain was a natural part of her biology at this age.

Author and historian Joan Jacobs Brumberg confirmed that other parents lack this wisdom as well:

> In our current cultural climate, we make little room for the awkwardness and special blooming associated with pubertal growth and development in girls. We prefer, instead, that our daughters stay irrevocably slim for their own sake and for ours. ("My mother weighs me with her eyes," an anxious student revealed to me about her well-meaning but misguided mother.)[11]

I did not then know how to create a welcoming ritual for this major change in my daughter's life, nor did I know how to speak out against the messages of "thinness" promoted in the media and throughout our culture. Did I, too, have the misguided notion that my daughter should remain "irrevocably slim"?

What I did know, from years of personal experience, was that diets did not work, but I did not have the words, the knowledge or the foresight to begin to help my daughter ease into her new body and effectively counter our culture's fat phobia and thin ideal. Linda Bacon, a nutrition researcher at the University of California at Davis, confirms the accuracy of my personal knowing:

> Diets, including the more "sensible" diet plans commonly prescribed by health care practitioners today, are a setup for failure. The human body is equipped with a built-in regulatory system that can help us achieve a healthy weight if we allow it to do its job. Dieting interferes with our body's

---

11. Joan Jacobs Brumberg, introduction to Lauren Greenfield, *Girl Culture* (San Francisco: Chronicle Books, 2002).

ability to maintain a healthy weight by triggering weight gain mechanisms and decreasing our sensitivity to internal regulatory signals.[12]

I had noticed, though, that the attention to weight gain appeared excessive during the travel abroad orientation evening. As we drove home from this informational meeting, Andrea swore, "No way. I *will not* gain weight while I'm away. I will be the exception to their rule."

I commented, "They sure made it sound inevitable, but I imagine it's a pretty individual thing. I say, don't worry about it." But Andrea did worry, and during her time abroad she made sure to lose weight, not gain.

Journal entry, November 2, 1994:

> I understand that things are different here. I knew that from the very beginning, but she's my pretend "mother"– not my warden. In my house [in Napa] I'm used to eating and doing things when I want to. I'm *not* used to having my mother act like my jailer. And it's starting to piss me off! I'm sick of being told, "Eat this! You have to eat that. Eat more. It's obligatory!"
>
> Fuck off! Leave me alone! I don't want to eat things I don't want to! And I'm scared to death to get sick now. If I do I get 6 kinds of medicines shoved down my throat! That's what makes you sick! I can't deal with it. I don't want to be stubborn or unmovable and I don't want to

---

12. Linda Bacon, Ph.D., "Tales of Mice and Leptin: False Promises and New Hope in Weight Control." *Healthy Weight Journal* 17, no. 2, (Feb. 2003): 24.

fight. But give me a break. This is the *outside* of enough! I'm never hungry.

It was the same in CA. Nothing has changed except that there I had a nice caring mother who understood me and here I have someone else's mother who doesn't understand me (literally) and is stupid! Yogurt and fruit are equal in health value for you but *no* I'm not allowed to eat one or the other. I have to eat fruit and *then* if I want it yogurt. I don't want to eat the fucking fruit! OK? What's wrong with that? I hate having her stand over me watching what I eat always wanting me to eat more. She doesn't do that with her kids. Evita can do what she wants, but me? *No* of course not! I am really! Really! Sick of it!!!

Once Andrea was accepted into the exchange program I basked in the glow of her efforts. I was proud of her accomplishment. My own insecurities allowed me to see Andrea's achievements as a fine reflection on my parenting and me. *It takes a pretty awesome mom*, I thought, *to have such a together daughter, especially at such a young age!* The shadow side of this pride surprised even me when just a few weeks before Andrea's scheduled departure she joined Jocelyn at the kitchen counter to chat with me on a night when it was my turn to fix dinner. After a few moments of idle chitchat I noticed a distant look on Andrea's face. Worried, I asked, "What is it, hon?"

With eyes slightly downcast she admitted, "I can't do it, Mom. I can't go. I'm too scared." I gave her the pep talk about how far she had already come, how this was the fear referred to during the family orientation night, that at this point in time it was a normal reaction.

Andrea countered, now crying, "I can't do it. I don't want to go."

I remember feeling a black anger rise in me. Bending over to grab a skillet from the cupboard, I slammed the pots and pans around as if to punctuate my words, "That is not an option. Look at all the people who have helped you. You will not disappoint them and embarrass me in front of all my friends and colleagues by quitting now."

I had allowed my self-worth to become tied up in my daughter's choices...what should have been hers had become mine.

 Letter home, November 21, 1994:

Dear Mom and Dad,

If I had the money I would call you every day! You don't even know!... I was feeling just sort of sad and lonely so I thought that I'd write to you.

Today was sort of a slow, sad, depressed sort of day but the skies are clear and there are stars. I found out that next week we have a different test every day and the week after 3 more.

Thankfully, Nov. is almost over. It's been a bad month. I love writing out on my balcony all skin covered and warm, looking at the ocean sky, watching people as they walk past going quickly and with purpose on their way. The cars humming busily. The trees are bare now. Ghost-like silhouettes against the sky. The winter constellations shining bright....

My daughter never again spoke of her fears around going to Spain. She maintained an outward appearance of confidence and strength. I believed the façade...but Andrea's self-assured exterior hid a vulnerable, sensitive child. I looked at her through the prism of my own frame of reference. I assumed my daughter's mind was constructed like mine. Somehow I could bounce back from the disappointments and challenges of life. My daughter would, of course, do the same. In my classroom, I was consciously aware of the multitude of differences among my students. Somehow, when it came to my own children I was led by my heart and forgot all that my head knew. Andrea was not me.

 Continuation of November 21, 1994 letter:

Sometimes I get flooded with memories so strong... not big things but the little memories of what our house smells like. And the wood-burning stoves and little things I used to do with you. And especially dinner. The smell of food, all sitting together, saying grace, talking about our day, and then if it was Friday watching a movie and eating popcorn and how Dad could *always* predict correctly what would happen next.

And sometimes the memories are not as good. Often I remember how hard I was to live with, though recently not as often as in the past. And the horrible things I used to be able to say and the way I was able to act. And even more recently, I think Dad can probably recall a few times during our week of camping he would have liked to throttle me![13] And now it seems so stupid! And I don't

---

13. Prior to Andrea leaving for Spain, Andrea and Tom went on a weeklong camping trip together on their way to pick me up from Humboldt University where I was attending a ten-day institute on environmental education.

know or understand how I could have ever been that person but knowing all the same that it's a part of me. Now it seems so natural and normal to clean up after myself. I get up–I make my bed. I change–I put my clothes away. I cook–I clean up the dishes. And it's not hard! So why did I find it so difficult before? And patience! It's not hard either! Well at least pretending you have it isn't. I haven't gotten angry or wanted to yell at anybody or just been generally disagreeable since coming here and it's sooo much better! So why not before? I don't know. And so now from the bottom of my heart because now I understand–For all the times I screamed at you and told you hateful things and wished I had different parents and lied and was selfish and crabby and didn't clean up after myself, *I'm sorry!*

And for the same number of times you didn't hit me, didn't send me away, didn't hate me and especially for never giving up on me, Thank you! It took a lot! I was not an easy daughter to have. Every time I said "No I can't" you made me see it through. When I was making things rough on you, you taught me what it really means to be somebody good....

I had celebrated the receipt of this letter. Andrea's words made my heart soar. Yes, she had come to appreciate us, especially when compared to the Castillo family, but when she spoke of pretending to have patience and of not getting angry, she was speaking of sublimating her feelings in order to fit in and please others. At the time, I was relieved that she had finally learned how to get *along*.

She apologized for all the "hateful" (her word) things she said. I would have been wise to respond, "You are an adolescent, a work in progress as are we all. Don't expect to be perfect. You're putting too much on your fourteen-year-old self." Yet, "perfection" was something Tom and I valued. "Good enough" was not in our vocabulary. Today, were I to have the opportunity to write it again, my return letter would encourage her to *feel* her emotions instead of pretending they did not exist. I would tell her that she had always been *good enough*, and that this is all we can ask of any human being. All the multiple aspects of ourselves are real and important, whether or not we or anyone else finds them acceptable. It was not a case of them being good or bad, black or white, but a continuum of grays, a continuum of all colors.

Two therapists, Mira Dana and Marilyn Lawrence, describe in the book *Fed Up and Hungry* how difficult it can be to see this kaleidoscope of colors, given the meanings a disordered eater often attributes to the words "good" and "bad." They say, "'Good' means thin, self-contained, always coping, never complaining. 'Bad' means fat, ugly, lazy, greedy, demanding and falling apart. There is no possibility of the good and bad being mixed and combined as part of each human being's nature."[14] When Andrea was here, I, too, had trouble seeing the rainbow within.

I did not have the consciousness necessary to help my daughter with the messages she was receiving from the culture

14. Marilyn Lawrence, *Fed Up and Hungry: Women, Oppression & Food, A Collection of Essays from Women in the Treatment Field of Eating Disorders* (New York: Peter Bedrick Books, 1987) essay by Mira Dana and Marilyn Lawrence, "'Poison is the Nourishment that Makes One Ill' *: The Metaphor of Bulimia." 205. *Title from S. Freud, *New Introductory Lectures on Psychoanalysis* (Harmondsworth: Penguin, 1973), 156.

in Spain—not unlike the ones young women receive in our culture. In *Reviving Ophelia*, an important book on the everyday dangers of being young and female, Mary Pipher points out the following:

> Girls have long been trained to be feminine at considerable cost to their humanity. They have long been evaluated on the basis of appearance and caught in myriad double binds: achieve, but not too much; be polite, but be yourself; be feminine and adult; be aware of our cultural heritage, but don't comment on the sexism.... Girls are trained to be less than who they really are.... Once girls understand the effects of the culture on their lives, they can fight back.... Intelligent resistance [using their voices and not their bodies to register displeasure with the cultural messages] keeps the true self alive.[15]

For my grandson, Fischer, I will be a *good enough* grandmother. I will work to keep *my* true self alive so that there can be one more model for him to witness.

---

15. Mary Pipher, Ph.D., *Reviving Ophelia: Saving the Selves of Adolescent Girls* (New York: Ballantine Books, 1994), 44.

5.

I Am the Cage—
I Am the Builder

Of all the liars in the world,
sometimes the worst are your own fears.

—Rudyard Kipling

Walking Andrea to the awaiting plane on the day she left for Spain proved extremely difficult. We held hands, and tears streamed down both our faces. We were saying good-bye for an entire year. My fourteen-year-old daughter would return to me a changed person.

Right before she boarded the plane she looked directly into my eyes and pleaded softly, "Do I have what it takes to do this?"

Just as quietly I recognized, "Not yet. But you will. Whatever you need to survive will be created within you, as you need it. Trust that, Anna Lynn." I patted her chest gently. "You have what you need inside."

Sounded profound to me. How much more helpful if, throughout Andrea's life, I had taught her what those internal skills looked like and how they could be accessed. When I raised my children, I did not have that knowledge. I could not articulate how one survived adversity any more than I could practice intelligent resistance.

 *Closing of November 21, 1994 letter:*

...I'm learning a lot about change too. "Quietly awed into silence by what I understand but cannot tell.... Borne by grace downstream where I see but cannot say."[16] My priorities have suffered an earthquake! The way I look, what people think...doesn't matter now.... I miss you a lot but don't truly want to be home. Sometimes on bad days, yes, but I still have a lot more to learn and a lot more to get out of this experience. I will admit, though, that sometimes a year seems like a *very* long time especially when there's something I want to tell or show you *right now* and I have to wait for the next phone call. That can be really frustrating....

I keep trying to decide what I want to do with my room upon return. All I know is, it involves a great deal of destruction and getting rid of stuff. I have to sort through everything, of course, but a lot's going to go—especially clothes. It's going to be so much fun! And please tell me we can *burn* the wallpaper! My room looks like a nursery! My only concession is that my Porcelain Dolls stay. I'm on the search for a really special Spanish one....

---

16. Robert Fulghum, *All I Really Need to Know I Learned in Kindergarten*, 147.

I've decided to have my own Thanksgiving celebration here. I'm checking out American restaurants—sadly—the best and most authentic I've found seems to be McDonald's. Rather pathetic really. I can always get a chicken sandwich (close to turkey) but I don't know what I'll do for the stuffing, potatoes, gravy and all the other good stuff. Could you send me my book titled *Heroes, Gods and Monsters of the Greek Myths* [Bernard Euslin]? I got Evita interested in myths but sometimes I get hazy on the details and every night I tell her a different one. It would be great if you could send *D'Aulaires' Book of Greek Myths* but it's probably too big and heavy—if so, no problem—don't send it. Muchas Gracias familia Buena! I'll try to make the next letter an upper! Keep your letters coming! I love you so much! And I *miss* you! Give my love to all and have a Happy Thanksgiving!

All my love! xxxooo Anna Lynn

P.S. Thanx for news article about smoking. Idea: when sending packages put a newspaper on bottom—good packaging and I like reading! ☺ ♥

Andrea's first family in Spain was a nightmare. Her host parents, the Castillos, were wealthy by Spanish standards. They, their five children and one grandmother lived in a three-story villa in a beautiful section of downtown Cuenca. Evita, their sixteen-year-old daughter, challenged the Castillos. We found out later that they had requested a female foreign exchange student because they were hoping she would be a positive influence on their daughter. As Andrea had told us in her letter, Evita's school had held her back a year. She smoked cigarettes, took drugs and had a boyfriend. Andrea landed in this family without the ability to speak more than a few words of Spanish (she had taken French during her first year in high school). Andrea liked Evita immediately. Andrea could see that her host sister seemed a bit "misdirected" but Evita became her lifeline in a foreign land. They shared classes at school and Evita introduced Andrea to all her friends.

Due to the language barrier, it took a while for Andrea to understand all the dynamics within the family. Because Andrea, as a foreigner, was novel and new, other youth were friendly and showed an interest in her, at first. With time, the fact that Andrea did not drink, smoke or do drugs prevented her from becoming a true member of Evita's circle of friends. Andrea cautiously acknowledged to us only bits and pieces of her sister's habits. She feared that if we knew everything, we would insist on her returning home. She did not want to come home.

Slowly, Andrea began to reveal to us some of Evita's behaviors, and a few of her own. Andrea admitted that she had tried tequila. She did not actually tell us about her experimentation with cigarettes and marijuana until a casual conversation with me just a few weeks before her death. At that point, it was a non-issue for me. Andrea's journal entries, which we did not read until after her death, revealed the pull of Evita's way of life, a way that provided excitement, entertainment, a means to relax and fit in, and lots of fun. It was also the antithesis of all that Andrea valued. This created a tremendous tension that became difficult for Andrea to reconcile. Once she began participating in Evita's lifestyle, she did not trust herself to stop. She needed help.

Shortly after Andrea arrived in Spain she requested guidance on how to "say no" effectively. She reassured us that the pressures to participate in drug use came from outside her home, but that it was rampant in Cuenca and something she dealt with on a daily basis at school. Tom and I shared all the strategies we knew. We then forwarded to Andrea additional information gathered from a local high school colleague who taught a class on peer pressure resistance. We even had a medic-alert bracelet made for her to wear. It warned of her allergy to sulfa-based drugs, but because it was in English, we encouraged her to use it however she needed. We reasoned that if students thought she could keel over with an allergic reaction to whatever drug they might be offering, they might ease up on the pressure somewhat. Andrea alleviated our fears by affirming that all our efforts had worked, that she was able to coexist with users of drugs without partaking herself. How naïve we were as parents.

Journal entry written in class, December 5, 1994:

I don't know what the difference was. Maybe it was because I had smoked and drank a lot more than usual. I don't know but I had so much fun! Our parents [the Castillos] are in Portugal hasta Viernes [until Friday] so on Saturday Evita and I went out until 10:30 then came home and had dinner and at 12:00 a.m. went out again. At about 2:00 a.m. we left for the Destroyer, a disco that was opening that night. We got there at about 3:00 a.m. It was Evita, Luz, Marisela, Reina, me, and the rest were all guys I didn't know (I knew a few). We danced and drank and smoked *all* night....

I don't know why it was different but it was like I wasn't invisible for the first time. I fit in a little more...and now it's like the same. When they see me it's ¡Hola! I'm not ignored. It's like I made an important step into being one of them. I don't know how. Probably because I was in a state of semi-consciousness all night—the effects of no sleep, joints and alcohol so I was totally looser. I didn't care about anything. I like it a lot. I think I had the best time of my life. And now that I did it once it makes it easier the next time to get into things. I'm also totally excited about going to Austria for 2 weeks. It's going to be great to have some time to re-group. I'm really looking forward to it....

My parents called Saturday afternoon. It was great to talk to them. They have their Christmas tree and Sunday Joc and Tracy went to help decorate. I wish I were there. Christmas just won't be the same. I miss it a lot sometimes. I sort of can't believe how close it's getting to Christmas already! I have to get presents for my family! I *can't* wait till Jan. 14.[17] I'm counting the days. It's my marker when things get bad. Another one is Christmas vacation. That's something else to look forward to. Bud E. Goat had to be put down. He was really sick. It's sad. I'll miss him—my walking goat, but maybe I'll be allowed to get a dog. I'm soooo tired. I'm falling asleep in class! I think that's about all that's going on now (or at least that I can remember)....

   −ALS

---

17. The date Andrea would leave for Austria.

Within four months of arriving in Spain, Andrea became very specific with us about the drug use going on around her and within her home, though she did not reveal her own drug use. She knew that we were her ticket out of the dilemma in which she found herself. She loved her host sister and did not want to hurt her. Andrea knew that the Castillo family home differed vastly from what she had anticipated as an exchange student experience. She was torn. When we told her we would call the program's headquarters in New York to initiate a move to a new family, Andrea begged us not to intervene. We agreed to hold off for a while and encouraged her to get things rolling on her end by reporting the drug use to the local exchange group, Cultura. By this time, Andrea feared the repercussions if she mentioned drugs. That conversation is imprinted in my brain.

"You don't understand," Andrea's voice tensed. "Evita, her brother and their friends—they all buy their drugs from the Cuenca mafia. The last person who told has been in the hospital for six weeks."

I remember the panic rising within my chest. "Andrea, do I need to fly there and get you out?"

"No, no, Mom. I'm not in danger." Andrea took a deep breath. "But if I go to Cultura and blow the whistle on drug use in my family, I could be."

I did not know at the time that Andrea exaggerated the circumstances because she did not want to mention drugs in order to get out of her home. It was the reason she wanted to leave, but she feared her participation might somehow be revealed.

Over the next couple weeks Andrea would vacillate on a

daily basis. One day she would insist that she needed to tell the local intercultural organization that she must be given a new family, and the next day she would insist that she needed to spend the entire year with the Castillos and just learn to deal. My heart contracted with heaviness and worry throughout this time. It never occurred to me that my daughter might be withholding information. I trusted her completely when she said that she did not use drugs. I could tell, though, that she could not see the darkness of her experience without an opportunity to get away for a few weeks to gain perspective. Similar to the way a prisoner identifies with her captors, Andrea defended Evita intensely. I did not view Andrea's host family or Evita as evil, but I knew that my daughter needed an escape from their influence.

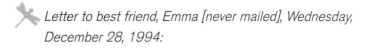 *Letter to best friend, Emma [never mailed], Wednesday, December 28, 1994:*

...I don't know if you understand this or not so I'll put it a different way. This isn't a poem or prose or anything—it's emotion:

The fear—The sickness of being here the sickness
of being there
Where? Inside—lose a part, keep a part, kill a part.
It doesn't grow back
The Anger—Break Out! Break Away!
What's holding you?
The cage is not within the place
I am the cage—I am the builder
Help me! Search with me

Let me share your secret world
Mine has kept me prisoner,
Understand—But don't box me into your parameters.
Take the whole of me—or nothing at all
The confusion—Broken
The box is dark, nothing keeps me inside
Yet I cannot find my way out.

I'm so sorry.... Now you know your friend is nothing but a jelly of terror inside, a good actress with an active imagination. Don't know what's happening. But I'm trying. I know I let you down. You, my parents, my family, everyone who believed in a different person than exists now. I'm sorry. I don't know how or why this happened—I was doing so well! And I'm still trying to pull out. Guess I'm a bit more depressed than I thought but this slip has been hard. I wish I had your courage around people, dear. I don't think you'd ever be like this, even in a foreign country. But then I wish a lot of things. I love you. Say hello to your family. I don't know if I'll send this or not. Might be better if I didn't. Maybe this'll pass. Love you much,
I *promise* to be more cheerful next letter ok?

"I don't know what to do, I'm always in the dark. I'm living in a powder keg and giving off sparks." —Bonnie Tyler

At this same time, a family from Austria, the Zagars, lived above Jocelyn in her college apartment building near the University of California at Davis campus. Bernhard, the father in the family, worked with breast cancer researchers at Davis and brought his wife, Gitti, and their two children, Philip and Martena, to the

United States to live with him during his one-year sabbatical. The Zagars planned to return to Austria in early January. They spent time with us the summer before Andrea left for Spain, and we had become good friends in the interim. We invited them to our Thanksgiving celebration so that they might experience a truly American holiday. There, I confided in Gitti my deep concerns for Andrea.

"Doris, you must let us help." Gitti spoke with sincerity in her lilting German accent. "We'll be home in January. Send Andrea to us for a few weeks."

The relief was instantaneous. Here were people whom I had grown to love and trust. They surely could convince Andrea that she needed to get out of the home in which she lived. I checked to be certain Gitti's offer was in earnest. "You would be willing to do that for us?"

She assured me they would.

I then pleaded, "Please, Gitti, we'll get Andrea to you some-how, but please—I ask you this as one mother to another—you must help my daughter see how damaging this family is to her."

Gitti promised she would.

 Letter home from Austria, January 18, 1995:

Dear Mom & Dad,

HI! I'm not in Spain so I don't have to say ¡Hola! I feel saved. This is like taking a deep breath—it's wonderful! So let me tell you about Gräz! It's gorgeous! My first day I got here and the Zagars had turned Bernhard's study into a guest bedroom. They had set up a feather mattress—down comforter and 2 down pillows—just like home! That's something I really miss a lot! They had a little table with a lamp, some tour guides of Gräz, a book about Gräz, a plate of fruit and a bar of chocolate. I thought it was so sweet! The next morning I went to town with Gitti and she showed me around Gräz a little so that on Tuesday when she had her hair done I could take myself on a self-guided tour and not get lost— Gräz is pretty small, don't worry! Then we came home and I went outside to play with Phillip and Martena in the snow!...

 Journal entry [while in Austria], January 19, 1995:

OK. So now I understand the problem—I was trying to fit in there. I was trying too hard to fit in and it didn't work because that's not me. I can't live like them. So I got depressed. Stopped going out. Stopped getting up and hated myself. So now I understand what happened and why it happened and now I'm sane again and everything's great. There's just one problem. Realizing all this I've realized something else. I don't like it there. I don't like anything about it. I don't want to go back. It's not my world. I don't even want it to be my world, so how do I go back and be happy for 6 months?

The time in Austria was as beneficial for Andrea as I had hoped. She was, at long last, willing to work on getting a different host family placement. When Andrea returned to Spain many obstacles presented themselves, the main one being that Cultura would not allow a move to another family for any reason other than drug use. Andrea felt forced to betray the host sister whom she had grown to love. Once done, Andrea needed to get out of the Castillo's home without delay.

The problem of where to put Andrea while a new family could be found was solved by a chance eavesdropping at the school where I taught. In the front office, before school, I was making a frantic early morning call to the New York exchange program's officials. Alice Cornwall, our site's new resource teacher, happened through the office during my intense conversation. When I got off the phone, Alice asked if I had a problem connected to Spain. I gave her an abridged version of Andrea's situation and this caring woman said simply, "I have a niece, Jeannie, who lives in Spain near Cuenca. I know she would be willing to help."

 *Journal entry [written in Spain after returning from Austria], January 30, 1995:*

> You are not going to believe this! Pen and paper *cannot* express the outpouring of joy I feel! Last night after I had gone to bed I prayed to God to let me have the strength and courage to find a solution, I prayed to God to help me. I asked him for his guidance and his help in my problem and today he has *answered*! When my mom told me that she had a friend whose niece lived in Spain and that maybe I could talk to her and have someone supportive here, I thought that maybe next month *if* she remembered I *might* get a phone call. But…today right now at 8:20 Jeannie *called*! I briefly told her my story and WHAM we're making a solution out of clay.
>
> I tell you if you want to get something done get help

from someone 20-27 [years old] or so. Jeannie already
reminds me of Jocelyn. At that age I guess they rule the
world and if they see a problem or injustice, *pity* the person who stands in the way of a solution! Already she's
calling Cultura to see how they work and get information
on how to get me switched and she's offered for me
to come stay with her if all else fails (which of course I
wouldn't but it's quite nice).

I am ecstatic. Nothing is promised and we might still
have lots of troubles but you don't know how *nice* it is to
have someone on my side helping me. At 15 [years old]
people don't pay a whole lot of attention to you even if
you say the exact same thing as someone 8 or 10 years
older than you! I prayed and I've been answered. It's nice
to know that somewhere up there God's on my side also.
Thank You Lord! Sometimes we really are given proof beyond doubt that *something* is watching out for us!...

Alice's niece, Jeannie Pascual, had married Pablo Alzugaray
just seven months before. These young newlyweds opened their
hearts and their home to our daughter. When Andrea returned to
the Castillo house to retrieve her things, her host mother greeted
her by slapping her hard across the face. The guilt that Andrea
felt for how she had maneuvered out of their home would follow
her for years after her return to America.

 *Journal entry, February 18, 1995:*

So—I'm out. I'm definitely calmer. I haven't thought too
heavily about anything that happened. I don't really want
to. I feel responsible. I used Evita as a scapegoat because

I wanted out. The confusion is with the half-truths—I did get pressure from Evita to do drugs but very little. She did do drugs in the house. It was not a nice atmosphere. The problem is I turned Evita into a monster druggie as my reason to get out when Evita and I were *best* friends. Up until I left she never really did anything except for use drugs and that became my reason 'cause how could I tell them the real one? I became my own enemy there. I don't know if I did Evita a favor or not. I think I did the right thing for the wrong reasons. It might help Evita and hopefully will help the Castillos. (They've got more problems than she does!) But it probably should have been done in some other way.

So now I'm with Jeannie and Pablo in El Escorial. They're really sweet and I like the apartment. Tango [their dog] is a cutie but relentless. He's an attention monster! So hopefully I'll get a family soon and get back in school. This is great but boring. I still have that displacement feeling. I think it's because this hasn't been quite what I expected. I'm *not* having a great time going to bars, clubs, dancing, partying and making tons of friends. That's not me. But I *am* having the most incredible experience of my life. It's a learning experience. I expected sort of a party carefree experience. But I think I've learned a lot. I'm not a naturally gregarious person. I make a few selective friends and greatly enjoy their company. I like clubs but not every day. And I *can* survive every situation. Just a few weeks ago I was miserable just wanting to go home but look. *I'm ok!* And I'm still enjoying myself. There *will* be lots of things I'll miss when I go home but it will also be nice to go home. Things are ok again.

So far this has been one hell of a year! So many things happened that seem worlds away. I've changed a lot but at the same time I haven't changed so much. I just broke down a wall and the person and things I wanted to be were always there. I've just finally started to find them. It's almost March! Four months left. That's all. Someday I'll be on that jet above the clouds going home again. Someday soon.

Andrea lived with Jeannie and Pablo for three weeks. Eventually, Cultura found a second family for Andrea. This family's lightness stood in direct contrast to the Castillos' darkness. They lived in Tarancón, a very small town about an hour southeast of Madrid and two hours southeast of Cuenca. José Luis and María Isidro Hontana Parra welcomed Andrea into their family. Their two sons, Rubén (sixteen) and Sergio (twelve), made wonderful host brothers. In fact, Rubén came and lived with us in Napa during the summer between Andrea's junior and senior high school years. Sergio was finally able to come live with us three years after Andrea's passing. Although they do not speak a word of English, María and José Luis faithfully send a bouquet of flowers to commemorate the anniversaries of Andrea's birth and death and a large box of her favorite Spanish candies every Christmas. They are a part of our extended family.

Journal entry [written in class in Andrea's second and final placement in Tarancón, Spain], March 7, 1995:

First day. Wow. I've got my second chance. I dreamt about Evita last night. I kept asking her to forgive me. I don't remember the rest. I'm out of the Lucas family home.[18] I don't understand the difference but it's here. My room, it's like bright and clean. The whole house is like that. The family too. When I think of the house in Cuenca it's like always in shadow, dreary. The family is really cool. They're like a real family. The parents listen to their kids talk. We all sit down to eat together and talk but it's like cool talk, important stuff. The little one, Sergio, is really sweet. He's so nice about letting me have his room. Rubén is cool too. He introduced me to some girls he knows that are in this school so I wouldn't be alone.[19] He doesn't smoke or do drugs and he's really sweet. The parents are really sweet. They're like educated or something. I don't know where the difference comes from or what to call it but it's almost tangible—something in the atmosphere, in the personalities.

...School's ok. The teachers so far are nice. March exams start Friday but I suppose I'll live. I'm liberated. This is the exchange experience I expected. Mercedes can go rot.[20] And maybe Evita can forgive. *No more mamá y papá.*

 Journal entry [during a lecture in class], March 9,1995:

Third day.... Why didn't I get placed here in the beginning? Emily[21]—you don't know how lucky you are. This

---

18. A reference to how destructive she felt her first Spanish family to be: My maiden name is Lucas, and there was much abuse in my childhood home.
19. Rubén and Sergio attended private school. Andrea was in the local public school.
20. Mercedes: the head of the Spanish exchange group who made it difficult for Andrea to leave the Castillo family.
21. Emily: the American exchange student Andrea's new family had hosted a few years earlier.

family. This school. It's like home. It is a home. It can be my home. Maybe I'll even learn archery.... *Help!* I've been put on the interrogation rack. Shit! This lady is horrible. Talk about being put on the spot. Get me out of here!!! Smile and nod. Try not to panic. Hide under the desk and maybe she won't see me! Oh please! This woman is horrible. Good Lord. Ok so maybe I feel better. No, 2 classes to go. Maybe I'll tell those girls I can't go out tonight. I need time to recuperate! Too many people. When I get nervous I don't understand as well. Isn't it fun to pretend you're taking notes??? This is a paper shuffle class, that's for sure. What's his face gave me that Greenday CD to listen to. He's sweet but P.E. teacher Martín was right. They're Tarancón's version of the "bad" kids. *Can't* fall into that again even if it's fun.... Thank you Lord the bell!!

 Ending paragraph of letter home, mid April 1995:

...And I think how easy it is to become a part of a family as great as this and how sad that we can't live in two places at once and how to divide your heart between where you want to be and where you want to go and wanting to be somewhere in the middle but wanting both worlds to stay the same. And hoping that you understand what I want to say without being hurt. The sun has left the sky and the first stars are coming out and I'm blowing you a kiss and wishing you goodnight. I love you lots!

Andrea

P.S. What's this about an all woman lesbian choir???

I'll be sending pictures soon!

Each of my many letters to Andrea throughout her year abroad ended with the words, "You are STRONG, you are BRAVE, you are PHENOMENAL!!" However, it takes more than supportive words for a child to construct feelings of worth. Andrea needed to be seen, heard, validated and accepted in her totality. We thought we were an open-minded family, able to allow our children to express themselves fully—this is certainly how others saw us. In reality, there was not room in our home for Andrea to be fully who she was—room for her to vent, and speak honestly and express openly every feeling she experienced without fear of rejection or reprisal. My own fears and inability to look honestly within myself sent out an effective, silent, blocking message: "Do not speak your truth." Words alone are not enough. Love is not enough.

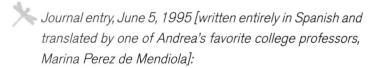 *Journal entry, June 5, 1995 [written entirely in Spanish and translated by one of Andrea's favorite college professors, Marina Perez de Mendiola]:*

Fuck, the year is almost over and it went by so fast, and so many changes. The biggest one (the most important one) is in the way I perceive things…only four weeks left but I do not want to leave! The other day I was thinking how, in the end, when I stopped searching for it I had achieved the goal that drove me to come out here and this allowed me not to deceive myself anymore. Moreover, I thought for a while that this year would have been better had I come [to this home] first but I learned a great deal about myself in Cuenca and the truth is that I do not have bad memories only painful experiences. But without these experiences I would never be who I am now and these were lessons I needed to learn.

I like who I am. I like my body now. I like my clothes and I like the options I have and that I am now able to see.

I have learned how to accept what I cannot change, what is out of my control....

It is true...the darkest hour comes before the awakening.

6.

Kiss the Stars and Hug Yourself

*Today I wear these chains, and am here
Tomorrow I shall be fetterless! But where?*

–Edgar Allan Poe

It was not until many months after Andrea died that I began
to piece together some of the hows and whys in the development
of her eating disorder. At first, I thought the illness began on
the day that Andrea made herself throw up. I now realize that
its beginnings came long before the first time she ever starved,
binged, or purged.

 Journal entry, early freshman year in college (17 years old):

...I need to be held. I am looking forward to going
home this time 'cuz I know that I can get hugs there. I've
never had to live so long without hugs before. I'm more
tactile than I realized. I'm not sure what I want, but I know
that I'd really like someone to want me and I want it now.
Once again, I'm studying, eating, sleeping, avoiding a

social life. Not letting myself see anyone as attractive is allowing me to live a sheltered little life, just like high school.

I guess I just want to know when it's my turn. Emma has a wonderful boyfriend, Caroline's been kissed. Quinn and Jacob show an interest in Keisha and no one even flirts with me. I'm exercising my ass off and trying to eat well and not too much and I'm trying to sculpt this body of mine into something marginally attractive, and I'm wondering Why? Why? when nothing happens. I was flirted with more before I left Napa. What's up with that? I'm everyone's friend but no one wants me for something more and I don't know why. Rationally, I know that these things take time but that doesn't stop me from emotionally wanting it now. I want someone else on this campus to care about me, and think about me, and want to be with me, and I want to find someone to feel all of that about as well.

Andrea was born into a family with a biological predisposition to mental illness. Not only did depression and alcoholism run in our families, but both Tom and I experienced our own physical and mental health issues during Andrea's formative years, beginning when she turned eleven years old. Just prior to the start of our personal challenges, Andrea suffered her own physical trauma.

One day after school, Andrea was playing with a friend in my classroom. Before sitting down to work at the computer, I watched my little girl pretend to be teacher with her young playmate. She used my long wooden pointing stick to guide her pupil in reading the words, one by one, of that week's poem. I chuckled to myself as I turned to face the computer. She sounded so much like me in front of the room.

Suddenly, Andrea screamed. When I turned around, I saw her clutching her abdomen. Her face appeared drained of blood as she yelled, "Where's the bathroom? I have to get to the bathroom!"

I figured she must have meant to ask which bathroom remained unlocked. Andrea spent many hours with me after school in my classroom; she knew the locations of the bathrooms. I pointed to the teacher's lounge and directed, "That's the only one open."

Before I could stand, Andrea ran from the room, still clutching her middle. I looked at her friend, sitting wide-eyed on the carpet. "What happened?" I did not feel alarmed. Andrea tended toward dramatics. I assumed an overreaction to an intense need to urinate.

Her friend held up the now broken pointer, "She tried to jump over the stick. It broke."

Something I had seen in my daughter's pale face told me I had best go and check things out. I walked into the restroom slightly perturbed at the disruption.

The room's one stall door stood open. Inside, Andrea leaned with her back braced against the tiled wall, her pants pulled down to the top of her hips. Her face was painted a ghostly white. Her hands trembled as she cradled her abdomen. She squeaked, "I'm going to die, Mom."

I softened. My daughter appeared truly frightened. I spoke

calmly and quietly. "Let me see, Annie." I kneeled in front of
her. When she released her hands, I gulped hard not to fall over
with shock. A gaping puncture wound, located directly above
Andrea's vagina, appeared like a newly created orifice. This
horrendous, jagged porthole allowed me to witness the pulsing
of my daughter's bowels.

I stood quickly and said, "Annie, you're not going to die, but
we need to get you to the hospital. I'll call the doctor. You're going
to be fine, hon, but you need to keep your hands over the wound."
At this point, I could see no blood, only immense ugliness.

I ran to the phone. Due to a nurse's harsh reprimands re-
garding an unauthorized emergency room visit with Jocelyn just
the week before, my mind was firmly fixed on the notion, *Get the
doctor's permission first.* My hands were shaking. I used two phone
lines, one to call the doctor, one to call Tom. I needed him to
come to the hospital. I knew I could be strong for only so long. I
would remain calm for Andrea, but needed to know that there
would be someone to whom I could pass the baton, and then
fall apart, out of my daughter's presence.

I heard Andrea's weak voice from the bathroom, "Mom…I
think I'm going to pass out.…"

I dropped the phone and ran to her side.

At this point, the principal overheard the commotion and
came running, and then everything happened at once. Time
seemed to go into warp speed. I flashed on the ridiculousness
of my attempts to call the doctor. My baby needed help. A true
emergency existed—if not, let the nurse yell.

Time at the hospital felt surreal. The on-duty surgeon,

Dr. Matthew, caused my heart to race. I did not like the look on his face when he examined Andrea's wound. As my fears escalated, Tom entered the emergency room. I looked at my husband's concerned face and felt as if my savior had arrived. Finally the burden of worry would be shared. He could take over and I could sit. My body experienced immense relief.

The surgeon was about to examine Andrea one more time before whisking her off for repair. Tom and I stood on either side of the gurney. I looked at him over the physician's head and shook my head as I mouthed the words, "Don't look." He ignored my warning.

Tom's face turned a putrid shade of green. With body slumped against the hospital wall, his eyes rolled back as his head seemed to loosen from its perch on his neck. Slowly he began to slide downward. The nurses nearby quickly grabbed him and led him to an empty bed just around the corner from Andrea's. Undisturbed, Dr. Matthew began wheeling Andrea off for surgery.

Andrea and I had been holding hands. As the gurney began moving, her grasp intensified and she begged, "Please, can my mom come? Please, don't make me go alone."

The doctor looked at the nurse. Nodding toward me, he queried, "How's she been?" He did not want another passed-out parent.

Silently, I prayed that the nurse would say, "Not a good idea." As my daughter desperately clutched my hand, I knew how much she wanted me with her; my knees were weak, though, and I yearned for an opportunity to collapse out of Andrea's view.

To my dismay, the nurse replied, "She's fine."

Andrea was numbed from the waist down. I spoke to her as the anesthetic took effect, and her body slowly relaxed. Her eyes lost their frenzied fear, but stayed glued to mine.

During the hour or so that it took to repair her torn abdomen, I laid my head on her chest with my body bent over the low gurney. Throughout the long ordeal I attempted to take my daughter's mind away from the surgical room. With whispered words I painted calming scenes from Andrea's life—Jocelyn's horse romping in the grassy field adjacent to our home, our goats frolicking in the backyard, our Araucana hens roosting in odd places, protecting their treasured blue and green eggs. Andrea's hand never released its grip on me, and I never once looked at the doctor's work.

After surgery, Dr. Matthew pulled me aside and admitted, "She's lucky to be alive."

What a stunning revelation. I knew the wound looked horrible, but because the doctor had not indicated otherwise, I had assumed no real threat to life.

He added, "She came within a hair's breadth of puncturing her bladder. She is a very lucky girl."

 Andrea, 18, September 1998:

> Some days I am beautiful
> the days my stomach is empty
> feel the bounce of my thighs
> feel the pounce of my eyes
> animated, amazing me

Some days I am not so beautiful
the days I am small and frightened
awaiting the discovery of my inadequacies
feel the protrusion of my belly
feel the shame in my smile
defensive, vulnerable me

Some days I am in control
the days I am powerful and experience joy
feel the breadth of my arms
feel the warmth of my heart
compassionate, organized me

Some days I am in chaos
the days I am overwhelmed and anxious
feel the nervous energy of my feet
feel the confusion of my head
frantic, scattered me

Some days I just am
the days I cannot even define
feel the vacuum of my mind
feel the ironic humor of my laugh
resilient, surviving me

This is only part of me
countless other days left to be described
this life is never dull, join me if you dare
feel the curve of my hips
feel the invitation of my lips
passionate, confusing, wonderful me.

Andrea had not completely healed from the distress of her own physical trauma when she observed Tom and me begin to struggle with ours. I worried about Andrea's response to my diagnosis of breast cancer. I consulted a therapist who specialized in family therapy. She warned me to be brutally honest with our daughters. Mothers with breast cancer were a hot button for her. She implored, "Never say you will not die. My mother lied to me when they diagnosed her with breast cancer. She said she would not die. I felt devastated when she did."

On an evening soon after this conversation, in our nightly bathtub ritual, I helped Andrea rinse her shampooed hair. She sat in the shallow water with her small, arched shoulders and head bent back under the running spigot. With eyes tightly closed, she bravely murmured, "Will this kill you, Mom?"

I knew my daughter's sensitivity. I knew she needed the assurance that I would not die from this, and yet the *expert's* advice made me question my desire to tell her that breast cancer would not kill me. As I bent over the tub and held Andrea's head in one hand and with the other directed the rush of water through her long soapy locks, I hedged. "It has the potential to kill, Annie. But you need to know honey, I want to live. I will do everything in my power *not* to die. I promise you that."

In the coming months, as I underwent intensive, aggressive treatment for breast cancer, Andrea's moodiness intensified. Her fear for my life erupted in blazing anger. She cried easily. On the day she attempted to smash the infusaport deeper into my chest, I knew my daughter needed help beyond what we could give her as parents. Andrea entered therapy and visited a counselor once a week for the rest of the year. I thought that therapy provided a means for Andrea to express her fears. Maybe it did, somewhat, but she still seemed to internalize a tremendous amount of worry over Tom and me.

Two years later a mass in my uterus was discovered. Following a complete hysterectomy, the pathology report showed the beginnings of uterine cancer. I entered a chaotic depressive state stemming from the many surgeries that were required, my fear of dying, as well as the sudden loss of hormones.

While I attempted to manage life without estrogen, Tom endured two traumatic events—the first, a serious car accident that happened late one wet night as he returned home from work in Sonoma, a thirty-minute commute. While driving the family vehicle, a Volkswagen Vanagon, he swerved to miss a car that had stopped abruptly and without warning in front of him. The heavy rains of the previous few days had softened the shoulder next to the pavement. Tom turned the wheels to the right, and the marshy edge of the road gave way into its drainage ditch. The vehicle continued its forward propulsion and bashed into a drainage culvert, causing the van to become airborne. A witness reported that the Vanagon made two complete revolutions before skidding to a stop upside down in a homeowner's driveway. Although the car was totaled, Tom survived miraculously without physical injury.

This accident, combined with the pressures of his job as an elementary school principal and worries over my mortality, helped trigger the second trauma, in which Tom hit an unassailable psychological wall and suffered a complete physical and emotional breakdown.

Along with severe depression came a mysterious loss of long-term memory. Tests of every sort were run. We discovered that physically, Tom suffered from sleep apnea, high blood pressure and diabetes. None of these illnesses explained the memory loss. Although we didn't know it at the time, Tom endured a heart attack around the time of his breakdown. We wouldn't learn of this event until five years later when Tom suffered a second attack, just two months after the first time Andrea made herself throw up. The physician conjectured that the original occlusion might have caused a loss of oxygen to Tom's brain, which could have contributed to his baffling permanent memory loss.[22]

For two years Tom suffered from the effects of the breakdown, unable to work. This time of upheaval, pain and confusion touched each of us at our core. I became an emotional jumble, Jocelyn and Tom sat in lots of denial—Jocelyn, with the assistance of teenage immortality, stuffed any worry with the blithe statements, "Mom and Dad will be fine. Just fine. Everything will be fine,"—and Andrea felt it all deeply…very deeply.

So here we have a child who at a tender young age was faced with the precariousness of life, who feared losing her parents, and who had a genetic predisposition to mental illness. We add to that Andrea's tendency toward anxiety and some obsessive behaviors, her extreme sensitivity and vulnerability, her black and white, all-or-nothing thinking, and an inclination toward

---

22. Stress and depression may also cause memory difficulties that can mimic dementia.

perfection. We combine this with her sometimes driven personality, her tendency to think of others before considering herself, and her depressed, also driven and perfectionist parents (one of whom dieted throughout Andrea's pre-teen years, modeled body hatred and exercised for the sole purpose of weight control). We plop this child into a media-driven culture that promotes dieting and a hatred of fat as well as unrealistic and unattainable body types, and *voilà!* We have a recipe for the development of an eating disorder.

The only missing ingredient was a weight-loss diet. Eating disorder researchers know that although not every diet leads to an eating disorder (and the word "diet" refers to them *all*, from Atkins to Weight Watchers), nearly *every* eating disorder *begins* with a weight loss diet.[23] As University of Virginia professor, Glenn Gaesser, tells us and Andrea's experience tragically confirms, "Body fat is not lethal, but the effort to get rid of it can be."[24]

Deprivation of calories—dieting—increases obsessive thoughts of food[25] and promotes binge eating.[26] That part of the mix—dieting—would come during the later months of Andrea's freshman year in college. But first, she needed a trigger, something to ignite this volatile combination. That something would come in the form of a college roommate.

---

23. G. T. Wilson, "The Controversy Over Dieting," in *Eating Disorders and Obesity: Comprehensive Handbook* (New York: Guilford Press, 1995), ed. K. D. Brownell and C. G. Fairburn, 87-92.
24. Glenn Gaesser, Ph.D., *Big Fat Lies: The Truth About Your Weight and Your Health* Updated Edition (Carlsbad: Gürze Books, 2002), 36.
25. Ancel Keys, J. Brozek, A. Henschel, O. Michelson, and H. L. Taylor, *Biology of Human Starvation* (Minneapolis: University of Minnesota Press, 1950), 126-129.
26. Gaesser, 34, 146-166.

When Andrea completed the Pitzer College registration form, she requested a foreign exchange student as a roommate. She wanted to give back some of the warmth and welcoming she had received from her second host family in Spain. Andrea's wish was granted. Mai, her roommate for the year, came from Japan. We met her during the move-in weekend. She seemed sweet, although much younger than her twenty years. This was the first time she had ever traveled outside of Japan, indeed the first time away from her family. She and Andrea became fast friends. The friendship lasted less than two weeks. Mai began making demands of Andrea immediately: She could not listen to her radio with Mai present, no phone calls allowed after 7:00 p.m., friends could visit only when Mai left the room and Andrea could not speak while Mai studied.

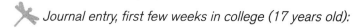 *Journal entry, first few weeks in college (17 years old):*

I feel like throwing up [refers to feeling nauseated; vomiting due to bulimia was at this point many months away], crying and being hugged. It's Spain—I'm back in Spain. College is not supposed to be this miserable. Shit, I feel like the bad guy here and I feel so guilty for not being able to make it work. I've been thinking of Evita too much. Different face, different name but I talk to Mai and I'm in Cuenca again feeling like shit. I spend as little time in my room as possible. I hate even reading in there. I'm suffocating—ironic that I'm dying for contact with the outside world for once. But I will not live in hell for seven months ever again [reference to the time it took to get away from her first family in Spain]. I can't do it. I feel that

I'm without an advocate. I don't even want to go back
there to sleep. Everything inside of me is shaking and I
don't know how long until it crumbles down.

Andrea called home for advice, "What should I do? She's
completely unreasonable. Every compromise I propose is shot
down. I'm at a loss."

We attempted to guide Andrea. It seemed that certainly
common ground could be reached. But Mai would not listen
to Andrea's attempts to work things out. In Andrea's next call
home she revealed, "Mom, it's taking me back to my first family in Spain." She became self-accusatory. "It feels like my fault.
I'm spinning into places of darkness, even having nightmares
of Evita again."

This worried me. Andrea really sounded upset. We advised
her to speak to her Resident Assistant (RA). Andrea attempted
the strategies suggested by her RA to no avail. Eventually, Jana,
the Dorm Advisor, and now a dear friend of ours, became
involved and attempted mediation. After two months, the
school moved Mai in with a different student and Andrea got
a wonderful new roommate, Madison.

A few months after Andrea's death, Mai's name came up in a
conversation with Richard, a friend of Andrea's who had worked
and volunteered in several places on campus during her first year.
His instantaneous reaction astonished me. He exclaimed, "That
girl was NUTS!" Andrea had felt so sure that a lack on her own
part explained why things had not worked out between her and
Mai. Upon hearing me state this, Rich rejoined, "No way! I remember everybody being amazed at Andrea's grace in dealing

with Mai." This tall young man shook his head in wonderment. As he ran his fingers through thick, wavy hair he repeated, "She was truly a nut case. I think she went through a number of other roommates before she was finally given a room of her own. I actually overheard someone say that of all the roommates Mai had, Andrea was the most patient and tolerant!"

I wish Andrea had heard that at the time it happened. The intense emotion caused from that event seemed to trigger something within her. She began spending a lot of time in the gym working out to avoid Mai. Once Mai left, the workouts continued.

Andrea spent time exercising with her Aunt Gwenn, one of my sisters, who lived not far from the campus. Gwenn showed her ways to increase the "burn." Andrea and her aunt grew close during Andrea's time at Pitzer, and I was thrilled that she had a mother figure nearby.

I started to wonder about the benefits of Andrea's many workouts, though. They appeared to border on obsessive. It seemed that they were no longer being used to relieve stress and promote relaxation, but as a means to lose weight and to counteract what Andrea had defined as *bad* behaviors. Andrea began talking about calories and fat incessantly. She started weighing herself each day. She spoke of the number of miles she would need to run to work off the food she ate. She began to cut fat out of her diet and then to eat less meat and even fewer calories. Andrea affirmed that she had never felt better in her life—she simply took getting into shape seriously. She assured me I had nothing to worry about.

I thought my daughter's first purge came on the day she made herself throw up. I now know that there are many ways to purge. Andrea purged through exercise long before the first time she ever made herself vomit.

I read an article in the *San Francisco Chronicle* during Andrea's first semester at college. A woman in her mid-thirties described in detail her descent into bulimic behaviors. It appeared that she began with the same behaviors I witnessed in Andrea: excessive exercise, counting calories, weighing herself daily. This was my first reading on bulimia, and it scared me. I immediately sent the article to Andrea with a gentle letter explaining my concerns. When Andrea received it, she called and thanked me and claimed that I had nothing to worry about.

Andrea did not begin purging by self-induced vomiting until the last two weeks of her freshman year in college. She told me about it the day after the first event. We enlisted professional help immediately. She returned home for the summer right before Jocelyn's wedding, and began intensive therapy the Monday after her sister's nuptials. Tom and I visited with her therapist, as well. Andrea attended sessions with a nutritionist, and a physician checked on her vitals. To help quell the desire to purge, she received a prescription for the anti-depressant, Paxil. All the "experts" agreed—Andrea would heal. We caught the behaviors early. Again, we heard that we had nothing to worry about.

I assumed Andrea could heal over one summer. I remained clueless about the amount of time it can take to alter the distorted thinking and change the behaviors that become habitual, in fact similar to an addiction, so very quickly.[27] It seemed, though, that a reprieve hovered on the horizon. Tom's unexpected heart attack in July of that summer actually appeared to be a mixed blessing. On the day that the surgeons wheeled Tom into surgery, Andrea and he made heartfelt promises to each other. Tom swore he would eat healthier and take better care of his body and Andrea swore that she would stop making herself throw up. Andrea kept her promise until mid-September.

There was a young man at college, Ron, whom Andrea had noticed. Although he was two years ahead of her, they had engaged in much friendly bantering during her freshman year. When she returned to school in mid-August for her RA training, this young man showed a definite interest. They began spending a lot of time together. Within three weeks, he called her his girlfriend and told her he loved her. Andrea became cautious but ecstatic. Unlike her sister, she had never dated in high school. In fact, when she attempted to find a date for the senior prom—she decided that she wanted to go to at least one formal dance before leaving high school—she was turned down. My heart ached for my daughter during that time. The first few "no" responses did not deter her. I saw such determination. At final count, six young men turned her down. Andrea went off to college hoping that she would have at least one date before graduation. To have a boyfriend, someone she really liked and respected, answered her prayers.

---

27. For those who survive, it can often take an average of four to seven years for a sufferer to begin the healing process in earnest. These illnesses are chameleon-like and tenacious. Vigilance and a non-judgmental attitude—from the sufferer, their family, friends and treatment team—are paramount.

Andrea, 19, exact date unknown:

I'm lonely tonight
Light one candle, make one wish
Look to the hunter in the sky
Orion, as solitary as yourself
Alone amongst millions
Stands apart, sounds like you

Feel every inch of self inside your skin
A beautiful ritual just for you
Exterior from the world for just a moment
Silver amulet, make me smile[28]
Tokens imbued with meaning you give them
Artificial but necessary

A fairy realm here on the floor
A mood to savor
Fleeting as your fairy friends
Soft, soft skin smells of honey
Build your cocoon and rock yourself to peace
Savor yourself, your softness
As hard as packed snow melting in the sun

Holding me tonight, Holding me tight
Yellow blanket, warm as the sun[29]
Safe and soft and close
My own private oasis
To share only with myself

---

28. Silver amulet: the silver, cylindrical, locket-like necklace given to Andrea by her sister, Jocelyn.
29. Yellow blanket: the Winnie-The-Pooh blanket also given to Andrea by Jocelyn.

> Myself and Orion, my hunter in the sky
> Never falling beneath the skyline
> With me on this silent night
>
> Kiss the stars and hug yourself
> And sleep in the bosom of your own endless song

As quickly as the relationship with Ron developed, it ended. Inexplicably, he stopped calling. He gave her no justification at the time. I can only guess at what Ron might have been feeling: The confusing contradictions of young love are not without angst for both genders. Undoubtedly Ron had reasons that may or may not have been honorable. But from Andrea's perspective, no explanation would have been good enough. This first heartbreak devastated her. She held the bulimic behaviors in check for another week or two and then they began again, but this time with a vengeance. The obsessive behaviors being expressed through her disorder did not allow for a quick release of the feelings she had developed for Ron. It took many months for her to pull out of this tailspin. By January, the light showed again. She went on a few dates with others and put her experience with Ron into perspective. And then, Ron returned.

As mysteriously as he had left, Ron came back into Andrea's life. As a senior, he planned to graduate in a few months and then go off to graduate school in another state. Even though time was short, he chose to reenter my daughter's life for the remainder of the year. Andrea was extremely wary. Though she was not willing to trust at first, Ron convinced her by begging for forgiveness and by promising not to bolt again. He called himself a fool to leave her. She trusted. Whether Ron lied, had a change of heart, or found himself overwhelmed by the complications of a relationship, we will never know. Two weeks before the end of the school year, right before finals week, Ron again began ignoring Andrea. Any progress made up to that point was flushed along with every meal she ate.

Ron discovered for the first time that Andrea suffered with bulimia when he attended her memorial service five weeks later. When one of my sisters asked him how he knew her, his response made it clear he had yet to come to terms with their relationship. He claimed, "Oh, we occasionally played video games together."

 Andrea, 18, September 14, 1998:

> In so many ways you are what I want
> But you are not what I need
> I realized, when I ask "why?"
> I am really saying I want you back
> tell me what happened so I can fix it
> so I can fix me
>
> NO.
>
> In so many ways I forced you to fit an ideal
> You approached me, and stayed longer than any
> You were big enough to block my vision
> with your embrace
>
> NO.
>
> I pretended it was a surprise
> but there is always a past

To leave, you have to walk in the door

In so many ways you are a landmark now
A pencil line, graphite gray on the column
by which I measure my growth.
Your absence empowers me
it surprises me, pushing me into new spheres
a group of phenomenal women

Yes.

They embrace me without adjusting me
Wise and vulnerable and honest about it all
They do not cover my eyes to hide themselves from me
or me from them.
Intimacy, cherished, beautiful again

Yes.

Be well, live well
Love
I will.

In many ways you are what I want
But you are not what I need

Yes.

I had forgotten all about the newspaper article on bulimia that I had sent Andrea. She reminded me of it months after she began vomiting. Throughout the illness, Andrea shared bits and pieces of her behaviors with me. At the beginning there were methods she used to force herself to vomit, although quickly it became just a matter of contracting her abdomen. It became so easy, in fact, that about five months before her death she began experiencing continual reflux—stomach contents regurgitated into her mouth without intent or desire, around the clock. It was an extremely unpleasant side effect.

Early on, though, I wondered how Andrea figured out the methods she used. One day, on a routine walk near our home, I asked what made her think of them.

Without missing a step, she replied, "Remember the article you sent earlier this year?"

My legs quit moving. I stammered incredulously, "*I* am the one who gave you the instructions?"

Andrea continued walking.

I uttered, "Oh, my God, what have I done?" I had not noticed the purging-behavior details in the article. They were all that Andrea *had* noticed.[30]

Andrea turned around and saw the look of desolation on my face. My arms hung limply. I did not think I could take another step forward. She quickly walked back to my side and, putting her arm around my shoulders, gently pressed me onward, assuring, "I would have learned on my own eventually, Mom. Don't take this on. It's not yours."

---

30. It is extremely common for pre-sufferers to get ideas about eating disordered behaviors from the stories of those recovered. For this reason, method details have been carefully edited from Andrea's journal entries and intentionally left out of this book.

7.

My Body's Ups and Downs

*Every person passing through this life will unknowingly leave some-
thing and take something away. Most of this 'something' cannot be
seen or heard or numbered. It does not show up in a census.
But nothing counts without it.*

—Robert Fulghum[31]

As we hung up from our desperate call to Jocelyn after hearing the news of Andrea's death, Jim and Karen walked into our
home. Karen entered the room first, with tears welled and arms
outstretched toward me. They told us that we had missed the
long-anticipated return call from the police by a mere ten minutes. Karen confessed that when the police officer stated that he
could relay his information only to a member of the family, she
had lied and claimed to be Andrea's godmother. Upon hearing
that the investigators had discovered a young woman's body, Jim
and Karen jumped in their car and drove, in the dark hours of
that early morning, to Napa.

---

31. Robert Fulghum, *All I Really Need to Know I Learned in Kindergarten*, 117.

Still seated on the footstool, I remembered an observation Karen had made a year or two before, about how she felt our family had the worst luck of any she had ever known. Her words had astonished me at the time. I had always believed that we had the best of luck—we all still lived. When I searched Karen's face that morning in the study I knew she, of all people, would understand why I felt compelled to ask, "Why? Why Andrea? Karen...why do these things happen to *us*?"

Journal entry, March 24, 1998 [18 years old—5 weeks before her "first" purge]:

I cannot believe how fast time has gone. In the blink of an eye my freshman year is six weeks away from being over! It is passing by so quickly and so many changes are occurring. I don't think I have really been able to take it all in. I love Pitzer. It awes me. I like the person I am becoming here. I am nervous about my final RA [Resident Assistant] interview on Thursday. I really want to get this job—it scares me a little though because I don't think I really know what I am getting myself into but I think it will be an amazing and challenging "learning experience." I hope I get the job but I will miss Madison next year.[32] We have really gotten along well. It might be lonely living all alone (if of course I get the job).[33]

...I love Spanish and my jobs and I get to meet Inez

---

32. Madison: the roommate after Mai, Andrea's first roommate from Japan.
33. One of the advantages of becoming an RA: a private two-person dorm room.

tomorrow at 5:30.[34] I am really excited. I think that we will become excellent friends. I hope that if I become an RA I will be assigned to Holden.[35] I really want to work for Jana. She is such an amazing woman; I want to be like her. Not entirely, but I admire her confidence and her frankness and I think it is great that she has waited till 32 to get married. I see her as a mentor and I like the camaraderie between her and the RAs. All in all I'm loving this college experience. There are bad moments of course but it is such a learning experience in so many ways. I think Pitzer is exactly what I needed. It's a definite God thing. ☺

After Jim and Karen's arrival in those early hours, Tom and I made our way to the living room sofa. Jim faced us sitting in the wingback chair with Karen perched on its arm. We four sat together in silence. Tom held me in his lap while we waited for Jocelyn's arrival. He chose not to wake his parents with the heartbreaking news, and so we sat, stalling, waiting for time to pass and hoping that maybe, miraculously, we would awaken and be released from our wretched nightmare.

I ran to Jocelyn when she and her husband Tracy finally arrived. Her wavy, brown hair, hastily tied up in a scrunchie, drew attention to her long eyelashes darkened by tears. With a

---

34. Inez: an elderly (in her eighties) woman that a friend of Andrea's in Admissions had helped over the years. The duties included visiting three to four times each week to help Inez pay her bills, run errands, buy groceries, etc. The friend was moving away, and Andrea had volunteered to take over these tasks. Inez had grown up in Spain, and Andrea delighted in speaking Spanish with her.
35. Holden Hall: the dormitory hall where Andrea lived.

look of utter disbelief, her concerned queries came immediate and incredulous, "What happened? Are they sure it's Andrea? How do they know for sure?" Then she declared, "I just spoke to her last Sunday. This can't be true."

I held on to Jocelyn while Tom shared the little we knew. When he finished, the time had come to make the call he dreaded. I sat, silent, listening, as he haltingly informed his parents that their granddaughter had died. I found it more and more difficult to speak. My bones felt stiff, my mind frozen in a surreal, Orwellian world. Occasionally, I rose to rush to the bathroom for the diarrhea, the result of my corporeal response, but otherwise I sat mute, unwilling to converse. I knew that if I opened my mouth, in place of words, my insides—my entrails, my guts—would spew forth. Ragged sighs, some deep, some small and staccato-like, were all that I could allow to escape my throat. My desire to remain silent felt instinctual, self-preservation in action.

After making a few more calls, Tom relinquished this duty to Jocelyn and Jim, who heroically took over.

Once the calls were made, Tom beseeched the room with bewilderment, "Now what do we do?" He appeared desperate for an answer. "There must be a manual, an instruction booklet, something…directions for What To Do When Your Child Dies." He pleaded with reddened eyes to no one in particular, "*What* do we do now?"

Jocelyn went into an immediate flurry of action. "You're right, Dad. There's got to be something. Tracy and I'll run to the library. We'll check out every book we can find on the subject." Jocelyn awed me with her ability to think. To move. To act. I sensed her and her husband's relief at the prospect of having something constructive to do.

Although Jocelyn dutifully returned with a stack of nearly a dozen books, we found no guidelines on how to proceed. She read aloud to us from the many volumes she had lugged home. We learned much about the grieving process, but nothing about what our next steps should be. We stumbled through the next few days, without signposts, without cultural guidance, without rituals to guide us in moving through the tasks that needed to be accomplished or to assist us in thoroughly, and without restraint, expressing our grief. We felt thrown into an alien world, one that is amazingly inhabited by about nineteen percent of the adult population in the United States.[36] Never would we guess the figure to be so high. And yet there is a dearth of readily available advice or guidance.

When a spouse is lost, one becomes a widow or widower. When parents are lost one is an orphan. There is no word in our language for the role one plays when one's child dies. It seems to be too horrific an experience to be captured with simply one word. Maybe this, too, explains the lack of primers on "What To Do If...." And maybe it is a method of keeping the possibility at bay. If there were guidebooks or rituals that would mean it happens, and not infrequently. If it happens, it could happen to me. Best not go there.

---

36. Nineteen percent of all parents ultimately experience the loss of a child. This figure includes all child deaths, from miscarriage through death of an adult child. Source: "When A Child Dies: A Survey of Bereaved Parents Conducted by NFO Research, Inc., on Behalf of The Compassionate Friends, Inc.," June 1999. For a copy of the study, please go to: *www.compassionatefriends.org/survey.shtml*

Journal entry, March 1998:

...I am proud of myself though. I haven't been eating much.... I've been pretty disciplined and I feel that the weight I gained over break is gone ~ I should start losing more soon. I need to be as disciplined about exercise too. If I can make it to aerobics more and hit the treadmill more and keep my food intake the same, I will start looking much better. I sort of lost the drive after the initial weight loss but I think that it's back now and I *will* look good in my first 2-piece bathing suit. I want my real weight to be how I look when I suck my tummy in. I have to burn the weight off. I am so sick of pretending—everyone believes it, and I can hold my tummy in all day if I need to, but I don't want to have to do that anymore.

Tom and I sat with Jocelyn while she made the arrangements for her sister's body, neither of us able to marshal the strength for this necessity. We chose to have Andrea's memorial service on the Pitzer College campus in Southern California because this was the place we believed Andrea considered her home. When we moved from Anaheim to Napa, Jocelyn was about to enter her freshman year in high school and Andrea had three years left of elementary school. According to the many parenting articles we read advising on such matters, these were the perfect ages to move children to insure a promising transition. Andrea, however, did not agree. Though only nine years old, she felt torn from her roots and bereft by the loss of a few special and dear friendships. Andrea also preferred the warmth of the area's climate and the flurry of its fast-paced life style. We vowed that, with time, she would come to develop similar companionships and sprout new footings in Northern California. Jocelyn and Tom believe she did eventually. I question that belief.

Jocelyn called dozens of certified and licensed services in the Los Angeles area looking for just the right one…the one that fit best with her sister's wishes. When she hung up the phone after her last call she exclaimed, "I've found it! Oh, Annie's gonna love this one. It's called 'Affordable Burial and Cremation'—ABC." Our laughter burst forth like an uncaged herd of wild animals. What release! It felt as if Andrea had joined us at the table with her wry sense of humor. Jocelyn repeated for us the conversation with the very kind but puzzled woman at Affordable Burial and Cremation:

"We have some lovely urns. They begin at around fifty dollars and go up from there. What did you have in mind?"

Feeling honor-bound by her sister's request just weeks earlier, Jocelyn inquired, "What's the cheapest one you have?"

Taken aback, the woman stammered, "Well, we have a twenty-five dollar black plastic box."

"We'll take it." Jocelyn could feel her sister's smile.[37]

A letter written to Emma, Andrea's best friend [When this letter was written, Emma had been struggling with anorexia for two years. Andrea's complete denial of her own condition is glaringly apparent—it was written one month before the first time Andrea made herself throw up.]:

Emma, Sweetie, why are you doing this to yourself? How in the world did you become Anorexic? You have

---

37. Andrea's ashes have since been transferred to a lovely golden vessel.

always been thin ~ where does this driving need to be thinner come from?

You are being dishonest. You, whom I consider nearly pathologically honest, are pretending. You are telling me what you think I want to hear and what you know you should be saying, but you don't mean it. You are holding this disease even closer to you and refusing to let it go....

If this were cancer you would fight it tooth and nail, if this were pneumonia you would follow the doctor's orders and be determined to get better. But Anorexia is not meeting with much resistance from you. The nutritionist told you to eat 2,000 calories a day and you're not. What is it about this disease that keeps you from listening to the doctor?

When will you be ready to hear that you are committing slow suicide? When will you be ready to do something about it? If I could make you get better, if I could fight this for you, I would. But Em, you got one of those that no one else can fight for you, that no one else can even help you with until you admit that you have it, and that you don't want it!

What scares me most of all is that I think, secretly, you kind of like how you look. You don't see the skeleton. You just see thin and hell, in our culture, there's no such thing as too thin is there? What you told me over break was BS darlin'. You are not ok with gaining weight, you don't eat whatever you want now; you barely eat at all.

I cried myself to sleep last night, Em, because I am so afraid of losing you to this disease and because, unless you fight back, I don't know how to stop this. Different continents, being away from each other two different years and college has not been able to pull us apart, but I am scared that Anorexia will.

I want you to know that you can never disappoint me, or your mom. We all love you unconditionally. You CAN'T let us down!! I *still* think you're amazing. I always will. Please be honest with yourself and with me. Stand up and fight this Emma! Fight the lies it sends to your brain about food and weight. Fight it because of you, for you, because you are special and beautiful and brilliant.

I don't know if these are things that you're ready to hear or if doing this is right or wrong, but if I don't write this Em I will be crying myself to sleep again. I have to do something. I love you. I support you. I admire you.

We arrived at our Southern California hotel at around one o'clock in the morning, two nights before Andrea's service. We made the drive down in Jocelyn and Tracy's larger vehicle to allow us to haul home the things Andrea had stored in my sister's garage for the summer. Tom and I would drive Andrea's car home.

Although family members had offered their dwellings to us, we needed to continue to be just the four of us. Before leaving Napa, we grabbed photo albums, pictures off walls, Andrea's journals and quote book, candles from her room, anything and everything we might need to memorialize her.

I remember my exhausted anger before sunrise the next morning when I felt brutally awakened by an intense, bright light. My eyes popped open to a room ablaze with radiant brilliance.

"Damn," I cursed quietly, my eyes blinded by the light. *"Why do drivers keep their headlights on when it's so early and people are still sleeping?"* Just as quickly as the bright lights beamed into our hotel room, the beacon rapidly retreated. I decided the driver apparently had determined the parking space outside our quarters unsuitable. I turned over, punched my pillow, then got up and stomped to the bathroom, grumbling about the disturbance.

My rustlings woke Jocelyn, Tom and Tracy. The light had not awakened them, but my tramping about had. Jocelyn flung the sheets back from the bed she and Tracy had shared and went immediately to the room's closed drapes. A bit bewildered, I watched as she allowed the tightly shut curtains to fall open, removing the hair clamps that were holding them together.

I puzzled, "Were those on all night?"

"Yup. We hate the bright light in the morning."

My mind was attempting to make sense of the blaze that had awakened me when Jocelyn flung open the curtains. I remembered. We were on the third floor. Directly outside our small balcony and stretching beyond to the building's rooftop was a large, densely leafed tree. There was no way lights, from any outside source, had entered our room.

Throughout the day my mind mulled over this mystery. Gradually, I admitted to the realization my mind fought to reject: Andrea had visited me that morning. I wondered if my cognizance would have been more immediate if her stay had been longer. This light was but the first of many sweet visits by my daughter's spirit. Her energy has continued to visit, especially during the writing of this book.

It was in this hotel room that we first read selections from Andrea's many journals. None of us had realized her talent as a writer. She had read to me a few of her poems in her final months, but I had no idea of her exceptional skill with words, the depth of her feelings, her tremendous insights, or pain.

The morning we left Napa, the coroner had called to tell us that Andrea had not choked to death as he had presumed. His preliminary autopsy had not supported asphyxiation. Tests still remained to be run, but it looked as if an electrolyte imbalance, brought on by purging, may have caused our daughter's heart to stop beating while she slept.[38] How could we make those who would attend Andrea's memorial aware that an eating disorder was the cause of her death? Late the night before the service we found the answer to that question when we discovered her poem, which begins "I have an eating disorder...." These were the words we would use in the program. Andrea wrote her own explanation of what took her life...she just had not believed that it could kill her.

 Andrea, 19, five months before her death:

I have an eating disorder
it is not had or did or used to
it is present tense

I am Learning
it is learning to love myself

---

38. Electrolytes are essential elements and chemical substances that are required for basic body functions.

it is learning to let others love me
it is surviving when they don't
it is that I damn well deserve that love

I am Trying
it is trying to listen to my body
it is about ups and downs and all arounds
it is trying to give myself what I need
it is letting others give me what I need
it is trying to recognize needs of others without
hurting myself

I am Going Slowly
it is being patient and gentle with myself
it is going through the day hour by hour,
sometimes minute by minute
it is not being everything to everyone not even myself

I am Accepting
it is accepting drugs as a way to heal myself
it is accepting the words depression, anorexia,
bulimia as tools to describe, not label
it is accepting the help and care and fear of others
it is accepting food as a necessity not an enemy

I am Beautiful!
it is beauty irrelevant of size or number or grade

I am Alive!
it is fighting to remain that way

I am Pain
it is trying not to hurt myself

I am on a Journey
it is laughing, crying, cartwheeling, eating.

It is o.k.

I am o.k.

Andrea's memorial service was held in Pitzer's trademark craftsman-style 1902 bungalow, the Grove House. This house had been one of Andrea's favorite destinations on the Pitzer campus. Its tucked-away location made it a unique stopping place. As a palm-treed oasis, the surrounding grounds are filled with clumps of native plants and shrubs, separated throughout by meandering pebble-strewn walkways. Dignitaries and Pitzer guests have stayed in its charming guest room since the house was moved to the campus decades ago.

Because of her love for opera, the service began and ended with music. We played *Romanza*, sung by Andrea Bocelli, as the first selection.

 Journal entry, March 26, 1998:

> Today is my RA interview. I am getting a little bit nervous. I found out yesterday that I got the mentor position but the one I want is the RA. Hope they come to the same conclusion the mentor people did. Eek!
> [Later that day:] Just finished the RA interview. I did a good job. I don't know if I have the job but I think I interviewed very well—Thank goodness for Bulletin Boards.[39]

39. Andrea had created a dorm bulletin board on breast cancer. Her silhouette of a woman gently cradling her breasts (two inflated balloons) had drawn much admiration and attention to her message.

I also found out that [I will be hired] as non work-study for Admissions next year. This was a good and exciting day. Thank goodness, as yesterday was horrible. I am so worried about Emma but I will call her boyfriend tonight and go talk to a counselor about how I can help her. I have a course of action to follow now. Things will be ok. I find out after the weekend if I get the job or not—My fingers are crossed.

Ran __ miles tonight in __ minutes. [Specific numbers have been removed from all journal entries.] Feels good!

With the introductory chords of music, a gentle, late June breeze billowed through the opened living room windows of the Grove House. This breath of air ruffled the petals and leaves of the grand floral arrangements positioned on various ledges and tables throughout the spacious, crowded room. The podium, the newly-appointed focal point, stood in front of the usurped center of attention, the room's prominent fireplace. Replacing the chimney's portraits, two framed photographs of our daughters looked out at the crowded space. One of our favorites showed Andrea with an impish eight-year-old grin, blond, crimped curls cascading over her shoulders, with arms crossed, standing back-to-back with Jocelyn, a beautiful and very mature looking fourteen-year-old. In the other portrait, the girls, then twelve and eighteen, again stood back-to-back, in replication of this favored photograph from their youth.

A lavish bouquet of purple and lavender flowers sent from Andrea's family in Spain rested on the majestic stone mantle. I sat on the front cushioned bench holding Jocelyn's palm with my left hand and Tom's with my right. Tracy joined us on this bench, allowing a tight-sandwiched row. Being cushioned among three bodies allowed me to sit without fear of melting into a still puddle onto the polished hardwood floors.

 Journal entry, April 3, 1998, one year prior to death:

> I got the job! Yeah! I got Holden as well. I am so excited. I'll work for Jana and have a double single [a private two-person dorm room]...it is all very exciting. Joc, Tracy & Mom and Dad are coming tonight for the Bridal Shower tomorrow.[40] I haven't gotten half of the homework done that I was supposed to—oh well. I worked out really hard though—ran and sprinted __ miles. It felt *good*. My endurance is so much higher now....
>
> I am looking forward to next year. It will be very exciting and Mom is going to come and stay the first few days I have to be back. We'll have an adventure!
>
> They'll be here around 1:00 a.m. and I haven't written my paper yet. Who knows when I'll do it. I don't feel much like working tonight—just listening to music and being alone.
>
> I got RA!

 Journal entry, April 6, 1998:

> Wow. A rather hectic and emotional weekend. [The bridal shower] was a fun party. I think Jocie liked it—she got some fun gifts and the games were good. It just felt like such a whirlwind. I was with my parents all weekend and I feel almost as if I barely saw them. I am tired and

---

40. A bridal shower for Jocelyn hosted in Southern California.

this morning [when they left] was kind of weird—we never really said goodbye. I don't know—I just feel kind of empty, the way I do whenever they leave. I go home in 5 weeks for summer and amazingly I'm not even really looking forward to it. I'll be working a *lot* and I guess I just really have finally gotten accustomed to life here and all of a sudden we'll be going home again, eek! I think I need some sleep and a *workout!*

Bocelli's powerful rendition of lost love floated through the air. Another light kiss of the wind brushed across my cheek. I closed my eyes for a moment and lifted my chin. I felt, in that instance, the unmistakable presence of my daughter. I breathed in her sweetness and whispered, "See how loved you are. Can you see, now, Annie?"

Romanza ended with the fitting lyrics, *"È già andata a dormire...,"* she has already gone to sleep....

The Claremont Colleges' kindhearted Chaplain, Reverend Catharine Grier Carlson, agreed to officiate at Andrea's service—Andrea had shared with me, after meeting the Reverend on campus one day, how impressed she was with this woman's gentle wisdom. We were blessed with her presence and her expert guidance throughout the service.

One of the first people introduced by Reverend Carlson was Steven Marks, the Dean of Students. He reminded me of a young Jimmy Stewart, tall and wiry with the same dusty brown hair. Steven seemed by nature a very caring, empathic human being. Although he and Andrea had not spent a lot of time together, he was one of her favorite administrators. She loved his easygoing, casual personality. His pain at our loss was clear.

Journal entry, April 12, 1998–Easter!

This was a good weekend. Saturday I worked in Admissions. It was really fun....

Saw a cute guy. The Pitzer security guard at the Grove House who came up and told us that the party would be on all night. Recently we've exercised at the same time. We've exchanged pleasantries. Seems really nice—also seems to be someone else's boyfriend. That's ok 'cuz in all honesty I don't even want to meet him or know his name—just look at him. It provides a little spice in my day and is harmless 'cuz we don't know each other, won't, and I don't have to worry about complications.

Reminder to self—think long and hard before you put yourself on that ridiculous emotional roller coaster of insanity ever again.

Ran __ miles tonight in __ minutes. Feels good!

From the podium, Steven spoke of a recent dialogue he had had with Andrea just two months before. He recalled, "She came into my office to chat, and during our conversation I asked her, 'What was the biggest learning experience you had as an RA?... What came from that for you this year?'"

Steven explained how Andrea had answered without hesitation. He quoted her: "Letting people have their choice. Giving people the responsibility of *their* actions, *their* choices, and *their* decisions."

He acknowledged, "That was *hard* for Andrea. Because, you know her, she wanted to fix things for everybody and help everybody. That was a real learning moment. That conversation came back to me this week and helped me put some perspective on this."

Steven looked right at me. I knew he repeated this conversation, publicly, to give his earlier plea with me validity. In response to my lamentations of guilt, of my inability to keep my daughter home, he resolutely held that Andrea would want to take responsibility for her choices. He felt strongly that Andrea would want me to allow her to own what was hers.

 Journal entry, April 16, 1998:

...On Campus Day was really fun. It is so amazing to look back and realize from whence I've come. I remember that day a year ago—I was ready to run. I was so uncomfortable and unconfident! Pitzer is giving me so much—so much confidence. I did a good job on the parent panel. It felt good to get so much recognition for that.

I'm going to visit Inez tonight and then I have to go running. I didn't exercise at all last night—yuck! I talked to Em last night—she sounds ok—not great, but ok. She has so far to go to fight this disease....

Four weeks of school left—wow! Who knows how that happened. I'm not looking forward to finals but soon all will be over and I'll be home for...The Wedding—even scarier than finals![41]

---

41. Although trained in opera and blessed with a beautiful voice, Andrea disliked performance singing. She had agreed to sing at Jocelyn's wedding as a reluctant gift to her sister (with much encouragement and pressure from me). This was a frightening prospect for Andrea.

8.

Eating Like Crazy

Life is too short to be little.

−Benjamin Disraeli

At Andrea's memorial service, I struggled to remain in my body. It seemed to vacillate between melting and floating. When it came time for Tom, Jocelyn and me to speak, no matter my efforts, I remained outside my skin. The three of us stood in unison and held on to each other. I wondered if those gathered to remember Andrea could see my dual presence.

Tom stepped first to the podium. After recognizing the health problems he and Andrea had experienced over the previous year, his deep voice began to crack. He pushed on in a different direction, "It is natural...to look forward...to reaching a particular destination...over the course of a life." Slowly and precisely he said, "In our conversations about what purpose we may have on this earth and our understanding of life...Andrea and I came to embrace the concept, that...the joy is in the journey...and we would say this to each other often. A few times a week, whenever there was a challenge, a problem, a concern, a terrific day, a new book: The joy is in the journey." With emotion, Tom proclaimed, "I am so thankful our journeys were simultaneous."

"Just three weeks ago we talked about the size of the universe...and postulated both how insignificant and how meaningful are the actions of people." Tom paused, regaining his composure. His voice quaked as he concluded, "Andrea's journey and ours have now diverged. No matter what size the universe may be, her stitch in its fabric will always be a joy to us."

Audible sobs rose from the gathering. Tom turned and hugged both Jocelyn and me. He returned to his place at Jocelyn's side, holding her hand.

I stepped to the microphone. Holding the sides of the podium, I willed my essence to return to the frame that had miraculously carried me forward. It was useless. My few simple words were uttered from an empty shell.

 *Journal entry, April 17, 1998:*

I can't concentrate; I wish I weren't working the desk right now. I want to sleep. That is how I escape so I don't have to think anymore. Grammy [Tom's mom] has a malignant tumor and is having a mastectomy on Tuesday—her right side. I'm going to church with them on Sunday and then will try to help out around the house. She must be so scared. She is 72 and has breast cancer—for the second time. I think she is scared of chemotherapy—I hope she doesn't need to go through that. The scariest part is that she had the type of cancer that is the most curable. It's not supposed to come back. If hers did what does that mean for my mom? I am scared. Grammy's mom died of cancer, Grammy has now had breast cancer twice and my mom had breast and uterine cancer. How in the world will Joc and I not get it?

I hope that everything goes ok, that this surgery is all she needs. Please don't make her go through chemo. I hope she tells me when she needs help.

Why do I feel like crying? What am I feeling? I want my mom. I want a hug. I want to be held and rocked to sleep believing that it will all turn out right....

Emma's anorexic, Gwenn's depressed and Grammy has cancer and I am sitting at a desk for four hours with nothing better to do than dwell on it. Thank goodness my mom is ok and healthy.

When I finished speaking, Jocelyn stood bravely before our friends and family and the Pitzer community. In a voice higher than usual, she spoke rapidly. She shared how we all felt tricked by Andrea's disorder—how none of us, least of all Andrea, had expected her illness to kill her. In an attempt to explain why so few of the friends listening attentively were aware of Andrea's bulimia, Jocelyn guessed that her sister's plan was to tell them *after* she had healed.[42] Jocelyn then poignantly shared a few of her favorite memories of life with Andrea.

---

42. Andrea had insisted that we keep her illness a secret. I now understand that this is a demand the illness makes: It thrives on privacy and secrets. Today, I would share my daughter's illness openly and with no more shame than if I were sharing about a life-struggling battle with cancer or some other deadly disease.

Journal entry, April 21, 1998:

Waiting for my laundry to finish so I can take a shower
and change into P.J.'s. Time is flying. How, how, how does
it go so quickly—do I get everything done? This weather is
beautiful. 90 degrees. Perfect for shorts and tank tops....
Must get will power in check—I'm eating too much. Last
night I binged...knew I shouldn't but couldn't help it or
just didn't care....

After Jocelyn, members of the audience shared the many
ways that Andrea had touched their lives. Finally, Jim took his
place at the podium.

Journal entry, April 27, 1998:

I had a goal to be __ pounds by the end of the school
year and I have not reached it. This is extremely prob-
lematic. So two days ago I decided to go on a diet. My
first real diet. [Andrea had been dieting for many months
at this point; she just had not yet accurately labeled her
behaviors] I eat no more than __ calories per day and I exercise. Hopefully, I can lose __ pounds in three weeks....
Today was my second day and so far I'm doing really well.
Will power! I *will* achieve this goal....

I'm taking Inez to the doctor's on Thursday.... I called
home today. Mom is really down. She says she's really
lonely and overwhelmed. I wish there was something that
I could do right now to make her feel better!

Grammy seems to be ok. I have to call tomorrow and
find out how her follow-up with her doctor went. I hope

she doesn't have to have chemo....
I'm worried about Jocie, too. She is so stressed. No
one even knew that she was getting nauseous and dizzy.
I wish she wouldn't keep things like that so bottled up.
She is so much like Daddy....
I want to slow dance. Close my eyes and sway gently
to the music—not with anyone really—just dancing with
my eyes closed in the dark, drifting, floating. A sea of air,
a bed of music—lie down on it, glide, peace exists in the
dark with your eyes closed listening to a country love
song. Strawberry wine....

So close was our relationship with Jim and Karen that Jocelyn had asked Jim to join her and Tom in walking down the aisle at her wedding the year before. Karen and I were escorted together to the seats reserved for the mother of the bride. There was no way Jimmy was not going to speak at our daughter's memorial service.

 Journal entry, May 2, 1998:

Two weeks left and drastic measures must be taken.
Why? Who knows. I'm getting my hair cut on Monday—
eek—why am I doing this to myself? Who knows—I need
a change.
...I can't wait till Monday at 5. I want my hair to be
gone. It is annoying me like crazy. I'm not telling my parents or anyone. I'm just going to surprise them all.
I was bad tonight. I ate all sorts of junk food. Oh well,
I have had seven successful days of diet, here's to seven
more. This week I will not give in to temptation. I was

good this past week, but I can be even better and I know it! Trade-offs—all about trade-offs.

Two more weeks, I can do it. It's going to be so nice to get out of here. Everyone is driving everyone else crazy! Here's to summer vacation. Three months to forget how much we all wanted to kill each other in the last three weeks!

Only 29 days till the wedding—wow!

Before turning to the notes he had prepared, Jim shared a sweet, extemporaneous story about how he had experienced Andrea's gift for dancing—together they had once wowed a wedding audience with their jitterbug moves. It had felt good to be cradled by the laughter prompted by Jim's tale. I felt keenly Andrea's delight throughout his entire eulogy.

When Jim shifted to his intended words, his voice choked a bit, "…I'd like to share a very unusual and beautiful gift that Andrea gave to me. As it's been said, in her sophomore year in high school there was this metamorphosis. And that was that Andrea went to Spain…a very, very, cantankerous girl; and she returned a very mature and worldly young woman."

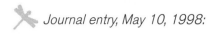 *Journal entry, May 10, 1998:*

I made myself throw up today. I have been sick for the past 2 days and eating like crazy. Today I binged compulsively…. I felt so full afterwards and I disgusted myself, so I decided to try it. It felt good afterwards, pure and clean…thinner. I feel much better now that I took the stuff I put in, out….

Okay, so I knew it was a bad thing to do, but at least it made me feel better. A last resort sort of thing. I have got to kick my willpower in the butt and be true to my diet from now on. I just have to remember to win this war against my body. I *will* do it. Do I know that it is sick and obsessive? Yes. But I also know that a disorder is the only thing that's going to work for me.

"When Karen and I first saw Andrea, upon her return...." Jim glanced at Karen, seated on the bench beside ours. Her stately, silver-gray head nodded agreement with what she knew he was about to say. "She looked a bit older, her voice had changed just a bit, and she had grown up tremendously. Doris kept asking Andrea to sing for us and finally she agreed. And so we sat quietly in the dining room and Andrea began to sing *a cappella*. And in that room..." there was a long pause while Jim collected himself, with emotion he continued, "...stood a young woman we loved, and out of her mouth came a voice from another world—an angelic voice, a voice that I had never heard. And this is the gift that Andrea gave me: She was barely through two lines of the song, when I started to cry. Tears rolled down my cheeks, and there were tears in Karen's eyes, too—tears of joy. I had never felt tears of joy...and until that day, I had never understood them. Now I do. And I thank Andrea."

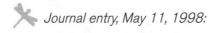 *Journal entry, May 11, 1998:*

I called home last night and told my mom that I'd made myself throw up. I guess there's still something inside me, residual from Spain, that refuses to let me self-destruct. So now I'm in the early stages of an eating disorder, and I have to do something about this obsession that's consuming my life. I compromised. I told my mom that I could handle giving myself this summer to lose the weight so that I'll be healthier. She wanted a year, but I can't handle that. I have to reach my goal this summer and privately, I'm hoping to do it well before August! How does this happen? It really is possible to create mental illness.

Reverend Carlson concluded Andrea's memorial service by instructing, "May none of us leave this place without understanding that we *can* cry tears of joy. May none of us leave this place without looking at the world with a bit more adventure. May none of us leave this place without knowing that our lives, the way we love, the way we give, truly can create a better world as Andrea did. We honor her, we thank her, and we make her perpetually a part of our lives as we do these things. Let us pray."

 *Journal entry, May 13, 1998:*

I'm a lousy anorexic. The __ calorie deprivation thing didn't work too well. I'm a lousy bulimic. I made my eyes bug out and called home sobbing and to boot I didn't even lose the weight I wanted to. I make bad impulsive food decisions and then hate myself for eating junk. I hate my body when I look in the mirror. Why is reaching this goal so dang hard? As soon as I go home it's all over though—Mom attacks. I'm hoping that I can exert some self-control these last 5 days and not eat any junk and stay around __ calories a day. I can deal with the aftermath at home this summer but I have got to undo some of the damage I did this past week ~ I was horrible. All I want is to be between __ and __ pounds. Why is that so difficult? To hell with body image ~ I can lose this weight.

Me (26) holding Andrea with Jocelyn (nearly 6) looking on in our kitchen just a few hours after Andrea's birth, on October 29, 1979.

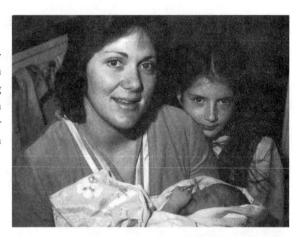

Tom, (28) holding Andrea at one month

Me (28) holding Andrea (2) after a swim in her Aunt Deborah and Uncle David's pool. When I was in the hospital having surgery for cancer, Andrea and Jocelyn made a montage of photos to hang on my hospital room wall—they wrote messages on the back of each one. On this one Andrea wrote, "I love you, Mommy. Get better soon. You'll fight the cancer. Love, Andrea."

Andrea (11) on Christmas morning. In the background is the gift from Santa she'd been hoping for: a blue parakeet.

Andrea (14), Tom (42) and Jocelyn (19) enjoying themselves on Christmas morning at my sister Jackie's house in Oregon.

Left to right: Our then future son-in-law, Tracy (22), Jocelyn (22), Rubén (19), (Andrea's brother from Spain, who lived with us for four months the summer before her senior year in high school.), Andrea (16) and me (42).

Andrea (17) and I (43) weren't able to keep our eyes open to see the end of the movie we'd rented. Tom took this photo and I remember hating it at the time—I thought I looked horrible. It is now one of my favorites—when I look at it I can remember how my daughter felt in my arms.

Andrea (17) Student of the month—Senior in high school

Andrea (18) with Inez, the elderly woman she cared for.

Andrea (18) and Tom (46) in her dorm room early in her freshman year.

Andrea (18) the maid-of-honor and the bride, Jocelyn (24) at her wedding.

Our last Christmas together—six months later
Andrea died.

I know that one day not too far from now it will seem long past but I write this now so I won't ever allow myself to forget the lesson. Life is precious, it is over faster than we can blink, we are never invincible. Truth is not eternal and human memory is as short as human life and I want to have this ingrained on my soul so that I remember that all of my life's moments are important and worth my full, wholehearted partaking.

A portion of a journal entry written by Andrea one week before high school graduation—using one of her favorite calligraphy pens.

Look carefully
Judge kindly
read under and between lines
the Journey is never so clear as the Destination
and the telling is more confusing still.

Last stanza to a poem written six months before Andrea's death.

9.

A Place Called Higher Ground

Never hesitate to hold out your hand;
never hesitate to accept the outstretched hand of another.

–Pope John XXIII

Journal entry, July 27, 1998 [while waiting in the hospital
as her father underwent open-heart surgery, two months
after Jocelyn's wedding]:

The heavy importance of words is so clear. He calls me his special one, his baby. He says—I love you more and those words have never meant so much as now. Interesting. Separate distinct regular words changed by the moment so that now when he says them they are charged with power, electric fear.

No matter how slim the chance of risk, that risk a decimal of a percent has taken over one hundred percent of our brains. Life has changed or is changing and we cower in the presence of the unknown.

Promises, what is the weight of a promise? Peace of mind? I have made my promise. I gave my word, an umbilical cord connecting us, feeding between us. Even in a drug-induced coma do we remember our promises?—So much solemnity, philosophy too early in the morning. The nurses so matter-of-fact, they see hundreds of heart bypass surgeries a week. There is nothing distinct or special here. Just a man, just a family, just some tears, just a bypass, but for us each minute is distinct, each second holds its breath. There is something special here, I say. My heart says don't take this man. Not this man who calls me his most special. The world needs this man. The thought of loss is so terrible that all thought is sacrificed just to block out this one. These surgeries happen every day. The surgeon has performed over 2,000. People survive these...no big deal—these are the words we are presented with as comfort. A shallow attempt—this does not happen for us everyday. Just don't think. Build a cocoon and crawl out when it's over.

To think that we walk around every day not knowing how strong those words are. They float through our heads constantly in the guise of the mundane and expected but in occurrences so unexpected the words crackle through the synapses crystal clear and crunchy at the edges. My most special. I love you more. That's why you keep promises. That's why you heal. I promised.

The phone rang around eleven o'clock Sunday evening, Mother's Day, 1999. One year to the day since Andrea's phone call letting me know that she had made herself throw up for the first time—nearly one year since Tom's heart surgery. I had just turned down the bedcovers and was surprised to hear Andrea's voice when

I picked up the receiver. Both she and Jocelyn had called me with Mother's Day wishes earlier in the day. Andrea claimed to be checking on how my day had gone. Although tired, especially knowing that I would have a hard time pulling myself out of bed the next morning, I snuggled under the covers for a tender long distance conversation. Which it was. Until right before we said good-bye. That is when I heard the catch in Andrea's voice. I knew, in that moment, that getting to sleep anytime soon was not to be.

"I'm not keeping anything down, Mom." Andrea's response to my "What's wrong?" was instantaneous. "I'm even throwing up coffee. It started with finals a week ago. I'm scared."

I jolted wide-awake. To this day I marvel that I did not think to say, "Go to the hospital immediately and request an emergency check of your vitals, electrolytes, blood and heart—I'll be there in a few hours." That did not enter my mind. Instead, my insides did a tight somersault as I probed, "Andrea, do you want me to come be with you?"

"I would never ask that of you, Mom."

"That's not an answer to what I asked, Annie. Do you want me to come?"

"Yes."

"I'll be on the first flight I can get tomorrow morning."

I heard the relief in Andrea's voice, "Thanks, Mom."

Before we hung up and before I jumped out of bed to make flight arrangements I bargained, "But, Annie, I have one thing I must request. When I get there, do I have your permission to find help for you in Southern California?"

"Yes."

✖ *Journal entry, July 29, 1998 [Tom was still in the hospital]:*

Mom spent the night here last night. Dad was in so much pain and it is just much easier for him if she's here. She went back home this morning to rest since they only got about four hour's sleep.

I look at her and I wonder how it must be feeling. She loves him so much and this pain hurts her heart as deeply as it is hurting him.

Interesting how we all come together at moments like these. Silently just gathering, supporting, upholding—love made tangible.

It is so hard to see him in pain—as big and strong as he is. There is something utterly vulnerable about him that makes me wish that I could take his pain into myself, as if I could withstand it better somehow.

Life in the hospital is like entering a time-out, a hidden niche. Time moves slowly and you can't think of much outside. The rest of the world is too distracting to contemplate and it requires great effort to remember the responsibilities waiting for you.

Day by day, little by little, so very, very slowly the cells repair themselves.

I promised him that I will not make myself throw up again and I'm keeping my promise. I have been so focused on him that I haven't really considered my food intake much—haven't been weighing myself compulsively. In the search for positives, Dad's bypass surgery may very well have cured my eating disorder. I'm not even dreading going back to Pitzer as much as I had been.

I arrived at Pitzer College the next day. Andrea had left a key to her room at the dorm hall's front desk. She had wanted desperately to pick me up at the airport, but I was arriving at the same time as her morning final. Her room was neat and tidy. Its fragrance spoke of her home bedroom—the sweet, musky combination of incense, scented candles and her favorite, dried lavender. I had not seen her room since before she had draped two sturdy cardboard boxes with fabric to mimic a squat television stand and coffee table. The newly added cloth lit up the room with black-speckled rain forest frogs of bright tropical colors leaping across a deep, electric blue background. Andrea had tucked a floor lamp into the corner opposite her on-the-floor mattress (sans headboard and frame, reminiscent of her set-up at home) to illuminate the conversation nook created by the covered boxes and a newly purchased burgundy dual-use chair/sleeping pad. Her small space emitted a welcoming, almost enchanted feel.

I had just set my bag down when Andrea whisked into the room. She threw herself into my arms and held tight. We were mutually thrilled to see each other, but Andrea's joy was two-fold—my presence and the completion of her last exam for the day. She still had three more finals to go, but the next one was not until the following afternoon, so we had the rest of the day to spend together.

Our time was lovely. We walked, we talked, we ate together, we window-shopped. Andrea appeared healthy and happy—the exact opposite of how she had sounded the night before. She alleged that my presence calmed her., that just knowing I was on my way had enabled her to eat and drink without purging all morning. I felt immense relief. I also felt powerful…like I could be the healing launch into wellness for my daughter. It was a heady notion, full of hubris. I believed I could save my child.

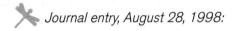 *Journal entry, August 28, 1998:*

> **It is time for a new chapter**
> **I am recovering**
> **I am eating**
> **I am happy**
> **Life keeps changing.**
> **What a delightful twisted maze it is.**

We spent our first evening together reading through all the material I had been amassing on eating disorders. Together we studied each page of the extensive resource catalogue I had brought with me. Andrea circled the volumes she wanted me to purchase. I planned to trek off for a Borders Books run the next morning while she studied for her final. When we got ready for bed, Andrea insisted that I join her on her twin mattress instead of unfolding the double-duty chair. I did not mind—if I rolled off the bed, the floor was but inches away, padded with a thick, wool throw rug.

Before crawling into bed I asked Andrea if I could give her a massage. She dropped face down on her bed, and wriggled her pajama top over her head. Her drawn out, "Suuure," told me she had been hoping I would offer. Slowly, I worked her muscles from head to foot. Andrea's toned body did not appear emaciated. She was slender, and I remember feeling immense relief at the absence of any telltale protruding bones. I did notice that the skin on her upper back was malleable, similar to how a woman's belly is loose after giving birth, but the skin did not maintain position in a way that would indicate dehydration. The rest of her body was firm and tight, loosening only under my methodical pressure.

My palms perceived her body's mellowing. The tension in my body relaxed as well. It felt as if I were ministering to my daughter's wounded soul. I had a strong maternal need to nurture her exterior—hoping that my rhythmic kneading could somehow stroke and lighten the sadness that was my daughter's interior. We both slept well that night.

 Journal entry, September 13, 1998:

> Well I'm hoping the worst is over. It is Sunday and I'm feeling better. I'm not nauseous and I don't think that I'll pass out today. After the movie at the mall yesterday I got really light headed and had to lie on the ground—very strange. I've been churning out poetry like there's no tomorrow—free therapy.

The next day I arose bright and early, armed with a list of titles of self-help books that would inform our journey toward wellness. In the bookstore, I took up residence on the tiled floor of the eating disorder section. Four hours passed without cognizant awareness. When I realized the time, books that had been opened in my lap fell to the ground as I launched myself to the pay phone two aisles over in the back of the store. Andrea sounded almost panicked, "Mom, where are you? Why did you leave for so long? My final ended an hour ago. Are you coming home?"

I felt terrible. "Yes, hon, I lost all track of time—you wouldn't believe all that I've found…so much. I'm buying about eight books, then I'll jump in your car and be there before you know it."

Andrea had hall duty that night. We squeezed together into the comfy swivel chair behind the dorm hall's entry desk and read a large portion of the day's purchases together. It was another wonderful day.

 *September 14, 1998:*

> Damn you!
> Damn you for making me hurt.
> Damn you for making me long to see you
> For making me recoil in pain when I do
> Damn you for saying things you didn't mean
> Damn you for saying you loved me
>
> Is there anything in my life that can be good and won-
> derful and not build character. I am so tired of being in pain.
> I chose to stop hurting myself—why did you have to?…

First thing in the morning Andrea went off to her second-to-last final, German. I was to begin my search through the phone book for a clinic, group or therapist in the area who specialized in eating disorders. I felt drawn instead to a title we had not had a chance to get to the night before, *The Monster Within: Overcoming Bulimia* by Cynthia Joye Rowland, a former television journalist.[43] I inhaled the book. Cynthia's story frightened me,

---

43. Since reading this book I have discovered many others just as beneficial, if not more. Please see the Appendix for additional valuable listings.

but it also gave me tremendous hope. Cynthia had survived far worse than Andrea for twelve years and she had still healed. I was ecstatic when I discovered in the final pages of the book a phone number for Cynthia's group, "Hope for the Hungry Heart." It felt "meant to be" because the phone number was the same area code as Andrea's. What synchronicity—a local call!

I was amazed when Cynthia herself answered the phone. When I told her I was calling for my daughter, Cynthia was direct. "That worries me."

I disagreed. "No, no, you don't understand. My daughter asked me to come here to help her. She's given me permission to do the research for her. She really wants to heal, she just doesn't have the time right now to do the leg work, that's all."

Cynthia proffered, "I'd feel much better if it were your daughter making the call and not you. She's most likely not as serious about healing as she thinks."

I continued to explain to Cynthia how she had it all wrong.

 *Journal entry, September 15, 1998:*

> ...Jocelyn is a good friend. I never knew that I would be able to call her that, but I'm proud to now. I love her.

I now recognize my pleas to Cynthia as the same ones offered by those who call for my guidance. How clearly I see the denial, the need for mothers to believe that their child is not nearly as ill as might be thought. That their child would never, *could* never lie to them. That their child has actually recently improved, just weeks after heeding their parents' ultimatum, "This is it! Stop these behaviors or there'll be hell to pay." The repeated refrains of their unrecognized denial, "Thanks so much, Doris, for all the resources you gave me last time I called. We got right on it, thank God, and now she's doing fine. She explained to me how this was just a 'bump' in the road for her. She's promised me she'll never do it again." And then the phone call a few months to a year later from the same mother, "She's started again, Doris. What do I do?" My unspoken guess: She never stopped. My heart aches for their naiveté—it seems to be a maternal need. My child is special. My child is different. My child is just going through a phase—this will soon pass—it is not serious. My child does not fit the mold.

I had the same unspoken need: As a reflection of me, my child is perfect. If she is ill in this way, what does that say about me?

 Journal entry, September 20, 1998:

It has been a week. Today would have been the trip to Disneyland. I am better.

I don't think about him as much and I think I have worked out most of what I feel about him.

What I haven't worked out is all the shit that this brought up. I have been throwing up again. I broke my promise—my honor code.

I need to go back into counseling. The promise wasn't enough. There are much deeper issues that I need to deal with to no longer feel the need to fill myself and then release.

I really liked what Jana said about having respect for eating disorders because they serve such an important function: of coming to your own rescue—of having the power and control to do that—of using it as a coping mechanism. It makes more sense than just calling it "bad."

I will call the counselor again tomorrow—hopefully he's there 'cuz last time I didn't even get an answering machine.

I am enjoying the journey though. I recognize that this process of self-discovery is one of the most important things I need to do. It is also important to me that I remember how this felt. I don't ever want to forget these emotions, not just so that I know where I came from—but so that I never take them lightly in others.

I'm learning that you don't have to be perfect in order to help others. You can be falling apart left and right but that doesn't take away your power—or qualification to help people. That feels good to me.

Cynthia spent close to an hour on the phone with me. Sadly, Cynthia was suffering from a recurrence of breast cancer when we spoke and did not feel hopeful about her prognosis.[44] Because of that, her "Help for the Hungry Heart" group had been disbanded, but she was willing to meet with Andrea and me if Andrea would agree. I guaranteed her that would not be a problem.

As I hung up the phone, Andrea entered the room. She was bubbling with excitement. "Have I got good news!"

"Me too! You first."

"Oh, Mom, you'll never believe—I aced it. It was amazing.

---

44. Tragically, Cynthia passed away in August 2004.

Not near as hard as I thought it'd be. My last final isn't till Friday, but let's celebrate tonight. After our walk, let's rent a movie, even have a mixed drink together." With both fists triumphantly raised over her head Andrea proudly cheered, "I aced German and we're celebrating!"

To accompany Andrea's victory dance, we broke out in simultaneous song. "Celebrate! Celebrate! Dance to the music!"

"You go girl," I shouted as our hands slapped a high five.

"What's *your* news, Mom?"

I didn't hesitate for a moment. I was positive that my report would add to the jubilation.

"I've had an unbelievable find, Annie. Before going through the yellow pages, I grabbed this book." I held up *The Monster Within*. Andrea reached over and took it from my grasp. She thumbed through it as I continued. "Wow! What a story. And Annie, I called the woman who wrote the book. She deciphered so many things for me. She even said you going to Spain could've been an acting out of your disorder even way back then."

Too late, I realized this was the wrong information with which to open. The change on my daughter's face was swift. It was like watching the construction of a brick wall in fast forward. First the mortar, then the brick, mortar, brick, mortar, brick—at lightening speed an impenetrable fortress rose between us. I had seen that wall before during her angry early adolescence, but it had been years since I had witnessed its creation. Haltingly, I attempted damage control. "She's willing to meet with us, hon. She's walked your walk. She knows what you're going through."

With a look of disbelief, Andrea skimmed the first few chapters of Cynthia's book as I continued my chatter. Andrea's eyes froze on the chapter entitled, "One last chance—behind locked doors." Suddenly, as if I had just kicked her in the stomach, Andrea fell back against her desk chair. Breathlessly her words rushed out. "This woman was locked up. Do you believe that's what I need? Do you believe I'm that sick? Do you want to do that to me?"

My mouth dropped. I had not seen this reaction coming. The entire room felt electrified with emotions. I stammered, attempted to back peddle, "No, no Annie. I don't want to lock you up. It, it's just that Cynthia could help us…she could help us find resources down here…she's in Pomona, Annie. Just around the corner…."

Andrea's body stiffened. This was the Andrea from long ago. The stubborn, obstinate attitude dripped through her words. "I will NOT see this woman, Mother. She doesn't know me. She doesn't know what I feel, what I need. I am NOT that sick."

Triage. I sat stunned, wondering, *Which claim do I counter first? Where do I begin?* I stared at my daughter's face, seconds that touched eternity, the tightening of her forehead matched by the constricting focus of my thoughts. A creeping realization converged. Cynthia had been right. Andrea was not ready to heal. I remember being dumbfounded; my head cramped taut with this newfound awareness.

In a slow monotone, my words finally came out, "You don't want to heal."

Andrea had left her desk and was pacing between the mattress and sitting area. She stopped and yelled, "You're angry.

Why can't you just tell me you're angry, Mother? Just say it. You're mad."

A small sound, a puff from the back of my throat emitted unbidden. I did an internal check. Was I angry? What *was* I feeling?

"I think I'm sad, Andrea. I think that's what I'm feeling. Intense sadness and disappointment."

Andrea again grabbed the book. She opened sections randomly. Disastrously, she read aloud some of the worst quotes. "I am not like this woman, Mother. How could you talk to her? How could you share with her what I do? How dare you!"

With this I jumped up and yelled back, "Now I AM angry, Andrea. I asked you if I could help. YOU gave me permission to do this. YOU said I could. What is it you want from me, Andrea? I can't seem to do anything right. How can I help you?"

"You can back off."

Now, I felt like *I* had been kicked in the stomach. Who was this person? How had I lost my daughter? What had gone wrong? I sat back in my chair. The rest of the words in Andrea's dorm room are a blur. Somehow we ended up outside, walking. We continued to argue, oblivious to the traffic in the street or the pedestrians we passed. My mind's eye can see us heatedly engaged, our hands flying, a bizarre circling boxer-like dance as we bickered, waiting for red lights to give permission for onward linear motion.

In vain, I begged Andrea to go with me to Cynthia, to give it a try for just one hour. I told her that if they did not click with each other we could leave. Andrea's refusals were angry and persistent. No matter how I tried, I could not scale the thick barricade my daughter had so expertly constructed.

 Andrea, 18, September 26, 1998 [after first break-up with Ron]:

I miss you
A jamboree of smells and sounds and tastes
touch me
your arms, big, keeping me warm
your fingers so curious.

I love smiling
up into your eyes, my happiness mirrored there
flirting and laughing...captured and silenced
by your kiss
your sense of humor, as warped and insinuating
as my own

I love the way you looked at me
awe and amazement and respect all in a silent stare
feeling so perfect, unfettered by bodily woes that
have plagued me my life
your husky voice as you quietly whispered
that you loved me

I love the dichotomy of who you are
a boisterous public persona at odds with a sincere
and vulnerable inside
the private you, warm and expansive, as soft and
comforting as a featherbed
your body spooning mine, your breath on my neck.

Utopia

I love your intelligence
knowing that you are able to answer
even rhetorical questions
an occasional fatherly correction of my grammar
your unpretentious, self-deprecating way of being right

I think I would love *you*
if you'd let me
even the part that keeps you frightened, backing away
but you don't allow me to make that choice
your fear removes me from your life,
and you from mine

For the rest of the day, we went through the motions of what
Andrea had planned. Like stiffened robots, we dutifully completed
our assigned tasks. I bought a canned mixed drink for us to toast
the triumph of her German final, which ultimately felt forced
and flat. We rented a movie. I cannot even remember the title. I
watched without seeing. We spoke very little. The movie ended
near midnight. Its credits rolled as Andrea, eyes fixed on the screen,
inquired, "When did you say your return flight was?"

I had not said. Like my daughter, I looked straight ahead
and without emotion stated, "I reserved for Friday, but I paid
full fare...the ticket can be changed at any time. Would you like
me to leave tomorrow?" I knew the answer to my question but
was unprepared for its visceral effect.

Andrea agreed coldly, "I think that's a good idea."

Dismissed. That is how I felt. You have served your purpose,
Mother. Go home now.

Journal entry, September 28, 1998:

Today is your day Little One…
…What are the things in the situation that really hurt me—why has this affected me so much?

• I feel that he took away my power. I had been in a really good place at the beginning of the year and he spun me right back to where I was.

• I allowed it to happen—I gave him too much control.

• I was so happy when I was with him—I need an emotionally intimate connection with someone in my surroundings and I hadn't found one down here. He became that and then he took it away so it hurt to lose the comfort and safety net I thought he was for me.

• I gave him too many pieces of me too quickly. I was too trusting and I dropped my guard and went in wholeheartedly. Although a relationship should eventually be wholehearted, I need to wait and establish that trust.

• He unmade me. I got annihilated. He sees me now and there is no recognition of what we were to each other. There is no recognition other than a smile and a nod. He banged me around but I didn't and can't dent him. For him, he needs to pretend that I am insignificant and replaceable and that is very painful for me to see.

• There will be no getting back together. He is going to need a *ton* of therapy before he can handle a relationship with *anyone*.

> Okay. I also have to remember that his reaction means I did things absolutely right. It was *real*–that's why I scared the shit out of him.
>
> I'm not going to classes today. I am being gentle with myself and doing what I need to do. Nothing that I need right now is crazy, wrong or silly. I need to feel the pain as much as I can stand, to work through it all and learn about me and it hurts....
>
> Do what you need to, Little One. Today is *your* day and so are all the ones that follow.

I did not know enough about the disorder at the time to realize how thoroughly my daughter's brain was devoted to the illness. I was not aware of the neurological and chemical changes caused by bingeing and purging, of the intense need my child had to protect the illness at all costs.[45] It was, after all, the way she coped with life. My daughter fit the modus operandi of a person suffering from bulimia to a tee and I was unable to see that fact.[46] At the same time, I fit the profile of a "mother of a sufferer," alternating between the controlling, manipulative descriptors and the indulgent, codependent, self-martyring characteristics. My ways were so subtle and covert that others would never have recognized them; not even I could see them.

---

45. Using scans of the brain, researchers have found that there are differences in the structure of the brain after development of an eating disorder. These alterations cause physical and behavioral changes. [Source: Bryan Lask, M.D., Consultant Psychiatrist, London, U.K., Conference session, "Understanding Eating Disorders and the Brain Without Really Trying," presented at the AED 9th International Conference on Eating Disorders, May 4-7, 2000, New York, NY].

46. Please see the Appendix for a listing of the possible characteristics, warning signs and risk factors of a sufferer.

I had a false notion of who I was as Andrea's mother and of my relationship with her. It took a good year after her passing for me to be willing to peer deep enough into my own psyche to more accurately see my self-deceptions. Like the skin of an onion, I continue to strip away the layers of my duplicity, revealing my denial, inaccurate projections, and automatic defenses.

I had access to none of these insights while sitting in my daughter's dorm room that evening. I called the airline, only to find they could not change flights after midnight. I needed to call back in the morning. I decided to call Tom first thing the next day to find out when he could pick me up before scheduling my flight. Although Andrea and I slept together as we had the previous two nights, this time our bodies did not touch. It was like lying on the edge of a deep chasm that had suddenly materialized between us.

At about three o'clock in the morning, the ringing of Andrea's phone ripped through the room's silence. Being in a foreign land, I did not know where to begin to search for the ear-piercing noise. Andrea's body shot upright and scrambled on hands and knees toward her desk. In the blackness, and with my body blocking her progress, it took multiple rings before the insistent sound was shut off with Andrea's groggy and still asleep, "H'lo."

I grumbled, "Who…?"

Andrea's body flopped back on her side of the bed as she muttered, "A hang up."

With no recollection of our wee-hour's disturbance, I rolled out of Annie's bed at seven thirty, still numb from the emotions of the night before. Long distance calls could not be made from Andrea's phone, so I tiptoed out of the room and trudged down the hall to the pay phone without a glance in the mirror. Barefoot and wearing crumpled pajamas I closed the phone booth's door, grateful that the windowed upper half allowed potential phone hopefuls to see the occupied status of the booth. A mother in PJs with hair sticking out at odd angles—better than a Do Not Disturb sign.

Tom picked up on the first ring. His voice sounded deeply concerned. "How are you?"

I relished his compassion just then. I had often felt alone in my fears for Andrea. I lamented, "Lousy. Tom, she's not ready to heal. I've been dismissed. I'm coming home early. I don't know how to help her. I haven't accomplished a damn thing."

"Oh, Doris, I'm so sorry. Didn't your sister call you?"

Confused, I answered, "No. Why? What call?"

"Sharon called around three this morning. I told her you were in Southern California with Andrea. I gave her the number. I'm so sorry to have to tell you this.… Doris, your mom died last night."

I screamed. There was no seat available. I bent in half, bracing myself with my stiffened outstretched arms and legs against the sides of the old wooden booth. I listened in disbelief as Tom repeated the little information that Sharon had given him.

The lens through which I viewed the world shattered. All plans, all thoughts became warped by this splintered vision. My shaking hands made it difficult to dial the phone as I searched for a family member who could give me details of my mother's death. With nine siblings (twelve total if including our much older and estranged half-siblings) it would seem that I could locate just one. After numerous failed attempts, I reached my brother Richard. He had been with mom in her final hours. Mom's hospice nurse had alerted the Southern California siblings that Mom would likely succumb soon to her battle with Alzheimer-induced pneumonia. Richard assured me that Mom died peacefully in the loving arms of three of her children and a grandson. He reported that Gwenn had tried to reach me with a warning, but did not want to leave the message on our answering machine. In a flash, I felt a surge of anger toward Andrea with the thought, *And instead of being with my mother during her final hours, I was battling with a stubborn, unappreciative daughter. How unjust!*

Back in Andrea's dorm room I sat on the floor atop her fluffy bedside rug and watched my child sleep. I wanted to allow her to wake gently on her own. The anger I had experienced in the phone booth just moments before began to dissipate. I realized that my mother would have wanted me to be with my daughter.

Andrea seemed to sense my presence as her eyes fluttered open. She muttered, "Mornin'," stretching both arms high above her head with a yawn. I tenderly shared the reason for my need to stay.

Andrea's profound grief and empathy with my sorrow allowed a softening of the attitude from the night before. We dressed quickly and headed to the funeral home. A few days later, Andrea joined the other grandchildren as a pallbearer for my mother's casket—four short weeks before they would be reunited.

Andrea, 19, October 1998:

There is a place called Higher Ground
When we get there nobody knows
Searching for it through the flood
We walk
Blinded to anything but the idea of reaching it
Higher Ground!

High School Graduation
We think we are there
But college is left to come
First Job
Finally we have made it
But other jobs lie down the road

Those who make it
To Higher Ground
Do not return to show the way
We walk against the currents in the flood
Seeing it in the distance

We do not play in the muddy eddies
We do not cry as things float past
Destroyed
Our eyes are fixed above the water

Surrounded by it
Immersed in this water that is life
We devalue, ignore, depreciate it
Higher Ground!
Keeps us slogging through
But we do not enjoy the journey

Higher Ground!
We have arrived
And realize the flood is gone
Life has ebbed away
Low tide

We look down
The masses still caught in the Flood
For the first time
We look into the water

And see...
The picnics, the funerals, the walks, the friends
The small triumphs, the pain of rejection
The first time we...
The Journey is the Joy

Higher Ground!
We have arrived
Life is done
Nowhere left to go

10.

Jekyll and Hyde, Me and My Body

*A life spent making mistakes is not only more honorable
but more useful than a life spent doing nothing.*

–George Bernard Shaw

It is not unusual for certain traits and trials to run through
a whole family, often affecting several generations. It was no different in my family. My brothers and sisters shared, to varying
degrees, the same dissatisfaction with their bodies that I harbored.
Our culture's hatred for fat and overweight bodies was mirrored
within my family. "Beauties must suffer" became more than just
a quip from our mother as she brushed through the tangles in
our hair. That saying unwittingly became one of our philosophies of life. So entrenched were we in the cultural ideals that
in earlier years some of my brothers chose dates based solely on
body type. Breast augmentation, an unbelievably popular but
intrusive surgical procedure, was seen as a valuable enhancement
by a number of my siblings.

Tom's family members, too, illustrated the power of our culture's thin ideal. Fat was as unacceptable to many of them as it had been within my familial constellation. Andrea's weight loss during her last year of life prompted a few family members to encourage her deadly behaviors with the all-too-common but strangely innocent observation, "Don't know what you're doing, but keep it up. You look great!"

I remember the times that I or another of my siblings shared with Andrea our "no pain, no gain" philosophy toward exercise and diet. I did not believe it could be harmful. "Pushing through the pain" during workouts was an often-stated value—again, one shared by many in our culture. Through books, videos, exercise and diet programs, the fitness establishment has done a lot to popularize the false notion that exercise must be hard, and practiced to extremes to be of value.[47]

All of us, even with our tremendous love for Andrea, were ignorant of the deleterious effects our habitual words and actions were having on her. We live in a culture that embraces and promotes distorted thinking about bodies, eating and exercise. Tom and I, his family and mine are all products of this environment. Sadly, this environment, combined with Andrea's temperament, genetics and dieting practices proved to be toxic for her. But Andrea was not alone in this. The

---

47. Glenn Gaesser, *Big Fat Lies*, 166. Exercise has become an acceptable, normalized obsession. A respected dietician/nutritionist once proclaimed in my presence, "I celebrate when an eating disorder is replaced with excessive exercise. At least that won't kill you!" Excessive exercise is not without its own dangers, and neither is exchanging one addiction for another (a physical death is not the only way to die) but I must ask: From what are we running?

number of people who are experiencing their lives in a similar way continues to rise.

 Andrea, 19, November 1998:

I am tired
And my head pounds with my heartbeat
My body hurts me
A mute reminder of the times I hurt it

"It"
I think of "it" as separate from me
Somehow
It is an individual entity

Is that how all of this happens?
Easier to harm an "it" than me
I can feel it through a fog
somewhere, it is here

When my head hurts, I hurt
When my stomach hurts, "it" hurts

I make "it" throw up
Not me, never me

When I take a bath I am pampering me
When I eat, I am feeding "it"
Maintaining "it" out of necessity

Jekyll and Hyde, Me and my Body
Separate entities endlessly attached
So good and then, evil

Andrea planned to come home for ten days at the end of the semester, then return to Southern California for a summertime house sitting job. She had made it sound like this was a serious commitment to help the Milhons, who would be traveling on and off throughout the summer. Andrea had agreed to watch their place during their weeks away. Because the plan to house sit arose just a few days after our confrontation at Pitzer, I suspected Andrea had devised a way to limit her exposure to home. We were beginning to threaten the bulimic behaviors in ways that frightened her. It seemed that she felt the less time spent together the better, and the more she would be able to protect and preserve her behaviors.

Before her trip home to Napa, Andrea visited my sister Gwenn to store her dorm room furnishings for the summer. Mini-microwave and refrigerator, computer and other odds and ends were tucked away in Gwenn's garage. I received a frightening phone call from my sister right after this visit. She was extremely agitated.

"Doris, Andrea's sick. She's really sick. She complained about the size of her thighs—there's nothing wrong with her thighs. Her legs are *thin*. We had spaghetti for dinner. I used the bathroom after Andrea. She'd thrown up the whole meal. She didn't even bother to flush! I've gotta tell you, Doris, I had a friend who nearly died from this. I'm afraid for Andrea. She's really sick...."

Gwenn repeated the thigh conversation and the spaghetti experience two more times before I had to ask her, "Gwenn, please...stop...I can't hear this again. Please. I need to hang up now. Trust me. We will talk to Andrea. My daughter's summer will be far different from what she's expecting."

My perception had always been that my sister was prone to overstatement, just like me. Nonetheless, her words left me reeling. I had to get off the phone because I could no longer breathe. It felt as if my chest had collapsed—there was no air available to me. Andrea's behaviors, when reflected through someone else's eyes, scared me immeasurably. I was weak with fear and terror at the abrupt and all-of-a-sudden realization that, if what Gwenn reported was true, Andrea's illness was spiraling dangerously out of control.

 Journal entry, October 2, 1998:

> ...I think about the night that he said, "You know what? I love you." I wish that I would have expressed what I was thinking when he said it which was—how do you know? That's a big word to use in a small period of time. Are you saying that because it's something you think you should say and I'll want to hear? Why are you saying this now?—what is your motive and why do you believe you're feeling it—if you do believe you are? I think that some of those answers and a memory of a dialogue from that would be helpful to me now.
>
> I wish that we had had longer—I guess I wish that I could feel now that it *had* been a relationship and had sort of run its course instead of feeling that it got broken off after this great beginning.

Once again, I called Cynthia Rowland, the author of the book that had caused such dissension between Annie and me. I told her how amazingly "right on" she had been in her assessment of Andrea's willingness to get help. Cynthia was not surprised. While attempting to contain my fear, I recounted the conversation I had had with my sister. I begged Cynthia for the name of someone we could call for guidance. She generously gave me the number of Dr. Frank Smith, one of the therapists in Texas whom she credited with having helped pull her through the illness. When I called Frank he agreed to do a phone therapy session with Tom and me that evening, trusting me to mail my payment for our session. We called Frank at the prearranged time. Not wanting to miss any of what was discussed, Frank allowed me to audiotape our conversation.

Frank cautioned us that Andrea's desire to house sit could be a dangerous opportunity for the bulimia symptoms to flourish unrestrained. Since at age nineteen Andrea was legally an adult, he knew we walked a fine line between pushing so hard that we would lose her and pushing just enough to give a message of concern and care and the need for action. "Is she going to have a lot of unstructured time?"

Unnamed fears tightened my throat as I acknowledged, "A lot."

Frank echoed my gut's knowing. "That's not good." He sounded as concerned as we felt.

Tom mentioned Andrea's apparent need to protect us from the degree of distress in which she found herself. Frank confirmed, "Yes.... I'm speculating here, but maybe Andrea grew up perceiving that she couldn't burden either one of you fully because of your own vulnerabilities. So now she thinks she's somehow protecting you by *not* sharing the depth of her distress."

"Maybe somewhat," I replied. "I think there's a lot of anger inside Andrea that's associated with our illnesses, anger that's never been fully expressed or even recognized." In retrospect, I find it telling that I could so easily see my daughter's unexpressed anger, but none of my own.

Frank continued, "Kids can make funny bargains in their minds to get a kind of sense of control, and sometimes they decide, 'I won't burden Mom and Dad anymore because they're on the edge themselves.'"

"Yes." This explanation fit my sense of the situation. "I believe that's why she's staying in Southern California, so she doesn't risk destroying our relationship."

"Well," Frank decreed, "you need to reverse that. You need to tell her that if she doesn't want to whack you all out she needs to responsibly get herself out of danger. She's misinterpreting how to protect you—totally in reverse. She's protecting you by putting herself at risk, going off wounded into the woods by herself where there are lions and tigers and bears."

Tom replied, "And yet she won't give up the bulimia."

"Yes. With all that's happened, she probably has emotions that are just intolerable to her, and one of the ways that she makes them not hers is in some strange way she makes them yours. Then, she has to protect you as if she were protecting you from feeling those feelings." Frank must have realized he had just gone beyond our comprehension and slowed down a bit. "I'm over-simplifying this—trying to get the point across." He patiently pressed on. "It's probably her own desperate fear of some of her own emotions. She experiences them as if they're yours because that's what she focuses on to separate herself from her own feelings." Later he emphasized again, "This isn't healthy adult separation. This isn't leaving home, enjoy, and all that stuff. This is pulling away and endangering herself." He sighed. "And these are the things that are so much more important than 'How many times did you binge and purge today?'"

Tom reasoned, "That all makes sense to us, and when we chat with her...sometimes it makes sense to her...."

Frank interrupted, "That's the problem. If she's left all summer with unstructured time, free to escape by herself, and she's on the border of getting really irrational...."

"Should we say no house sitting?" My brain was on overload. What was he saying? What EXACTLY did we need to say to our daughter? I wanted desperately for Frank to just give us the words, to tell us directly what to do.

"I would think she needs to be home and with that therapist she already connected with. One reason I do this work is that there are sufferers complaining they can't find therapists who will quit talking about how many times they binged and purged and what they're eating, and instead talk about life and why they feel like they're dying."[48]

---

48. I now understand the necessity of immediately dealing with behaviors. A body must be hydrated and fed so that rational thought is possible. Once the individual's body is stabilized, then distorted thinking can be addressed. Although continued attention must be given to reducing the frequency of the behaviors, they are often the last symptom to leave. This also points to why a team approach, including an individual therapist, a family therapist, group therapy, a health care provider and nutritionist, all well-versed in a non-dieting approach to wellness and communicating with each other regularly, is so very important for optimum treatment. Effectively treating eating disorders is an extremely tall order for one lone therapist to fill.

Tom asserted, "Nothing will change until she decides and is willing. If we say, 'You get help or...'"

Frank inserted, "Mainly the advantage of coming home is she doesn't *have* to give up everything else—forfeit it—she can go to school locally and maintain her pace through school while she pursues help responsibly." He paused and then added, "What I fear is she is on the edge of endangerment in terms of spilling over into other symptoms that can start becoming habitual and take her further out of rationality."

I repeated for Frank the phone call I had received from Andrea late one mid-November night. Memory of that fervent verbal exchange is ever-present, the time when the pause in our conversation came and I urged, "What's wrong?" and Andrea did not answer. After a long silence, I whispered, "You cut yourself, didn't you?" Just that day, I had read an article about how disordered eating behaviors can lead to other symptoms, cutting among them. I think Andrea was as surprised as I that my guess was accurate—in a moment of intense pain she had cut two thin lines on the inside of her left forearm.

I remember thinking that this was too much, this behavior had to stop. We talked long into the night. I lectured—giving the most impassioned rejoinders I could muster—at one point declaring, "This is bullshit, Annie! YOU are the one who can choose to stop the escalation of your behaviors!" When we finally finished, I felt thoroughly emptied. My daughter claimed that I had "saved her from herself." Again my hubris...I, too, believed that to be true. Andrea never cut again, but I could not save my daughter.

Frank breathed deeply. "What you're working with here is…is her not being willing to get help."

Not willing to get help. I was reminded how this realization had just crystallized for me during our confrontation the week before. Our nearly two-hour session with Frank validated our need to have a serious discussion with Andrea. We could not allow her to house sit for the summer. Using what we had just learned from Frank, we carefully crafted the discourse we would have with our daughter. We wrote down our words because we wanted to be certain that we expressed what we meant with love and without leaving anything out. Many of the words were direct quotes from Frank. At the time we did not fully understand the reality of much of what we said, nor did we truly believe that our daughter was in danger of dying. But Frank insisted that we had to present it to Andrea as if that was exactly what we believed.

 Journal entry, October 25, 1998:

…I broke down. I went home early for fall break. I saw [my therapist] a lot. It helped…. Life got too much for me to handle, but I have constricted my world a little and am in more control again. I am down to 3 classes, I'm withdrawing from CODE [Claremont's Coalition on Disordered Eating—Andrea was recommended by the Dean, who was unaware of her disorder, as a fine volunteer for this organization] and finding someone else to help with Inez [the elderly woman Andrea cared for]…. I went to hell and back again but I still made it back.

…I turn 19 on Thursday. Sometimes I feel like so

much has been crammed into such a short period of time.
I live an amazing life!

So, on Thursday I begin another year of this amazing
journey. Ron is being slowly put in my past, Spain has
been brought to the surface so she can finally sink down
where she belongs and I am learning to reach out and
connect with people and take care of myself. If I can't love
me and my body how can I expect to love anyone else
and know I deserve their love? Good question.

What do I need to learn from my experience of grieving Ron?

So far, this is what I think:

Grieve as long as you need to, no one can tell you
how much or how long you should hurt.

Even though in the future you want to be cautious
and move much slower—don't get jaded—yes you can get
hurt but you can heal and if he's worth being with at all
he's worth being with wholeheartedly.

Be honest about your emotions with yourself and others. Address them immediately. You're not wrong.

Go as deep into the joy and as deep into the pain as
you can stand and while you're there—look around—figure
out what you see.

To everything there is a purpose and a reason for
each experience we have. There is a depth to the universe
which is profound and extends far deeper than the pain
you feel now—circling back around until there is a time in
the future when that experience, that lesson is needed
and useful—not painful but beautiful. Search for the lessons. They are the roadmaps for tomorrow.

Two days after our conversation with Frank Smith, Andrea made the long drive home from Southern California. When she walked in the door late that evening she appeared jubilant, all of the testiness and anger that had been a part of our time together back at Pitzer—gone. She threw her arms around us and hugged with the glee of a youthful, healthy student's "end of finals, beginning of summer" exuberance.

If Andrea's delight was an eight on a scale of one to ten, in contrast, our feelings were somewhere around a minus two. Our thrill to see her safely home was real, but we had to force our faces to smile. She did not seem to notice. After helping to unload her car, Andrea began sorting through the many boxes and piles that we had assisted in carrying into her bedroom. The clothes from her dorm closet had been transported on their hangers and piled neatly on top of everything else. She began the unpacking ritual by disentangling the hangers and returning them to their home closet, chatting all the while about her plans for the next day.

"I so want to go to the mall with you, Mom. I need a bathing suit for the summer—my first two-piece!" She threw a "yes!" fist jab to the air before continuing, "The whole drive home I kept thinking about the fun we'll have. Let's walk to Starbucks in the morning for mochas before heading to the center. It's been forever since we've gone shopping to actually *buy* something. I can't wait!"

As Andrea returned her room to its previously inhabited state, I went in search of Tom. Exhausted from the emotional drain of the last two days, he'd headed to bed early. Although nearly a year had passed since his heart attack and quintuple bypass, his recovery had been intertwined with the progression of Andrea's illness—he continued to tire easily. I found him before he went to sleep. My conscience couldn't take the feel of deception caused by our forced, happy exteriors.

"I know we agreed to give her tonight to settle in, and talk with her in the morning," I explained, "but Tom, she's all excited about the day she's planned for tomorrow. It feels cruel to spring this on her after 'pretending' all was okay tonight. Are you willing to have the talk now?"

Through his weariness, Tom yielded. "But give her a choice, Doris. She may be too wiped out to want to talk tonight." His voice reflected the fatigue of his body as he pulled himself to a seated position, reaching for our prepared script from the corner of his dresser.

Andrea reacted calmly to my query. "If you and Daddy have something to tell me, Mom, I'd rather hear it sooner than later. Let's talk now."

We joined Tom in the bedroom. I sat on my side of the bed, and Andrea tucked her legs under her on the padded cedar chest at the foot of our bed. To her credit, Andrea listened to our monologue with patience and respect. Frank Smith had instructed that Tom be responsible for delivering the lion's share of the message since disordered eaters often feel abandoned by their fathers. We explained to Andrea our need for a script, but did not mention our conversation with Frank. We did not want her to disregard our words because of their extended connection with the author that Andrea had so thoroughly rejected.

With loving firmness, Tom began, "Andrea, your mother and I are deeply concerned about you." He read the words we had scribed the night before:

> It appears to us that you are practicing a life-threatening addiction. We want to go on record standing for the truth that you will not look at right now. We want to make sure you don't have the luxury of our reliable absence or our silence as an unspoken agreement with what you're doing.

Barely glancing at our notes, Tom held eye contact with Andrea. Her eyes never left his. He went on to tell her about the dangers of unstructured time and about the denial she was in and her inability to deal honestly with the bulimia. He continued,

> You are coping with something that's devouring you...with the notion that you're in control of it and want to protect it—it is something you are anchored to—to try and keep the inner world that you won't look into under control.

Andrea's body was still, her face without expression. Tom's voice remained even and firm.

> You are vulnerable right now—you are at a place where you could easily escalate into other symptoms.
> You feel you can't burden us—that we're on the edge—but you've misinterpreted our message. What makes us crazy is *not knowing* and:
>
> your isolation...
> your not getting serious help...

your not trusting us…
your not wanting to be connected…
your disconnecting from us when that's the last thing
you need…
your pulling away and endangering yourself…
the agony for us of not knowing your intentions on
any given day.

Tom took a deep breath and concluded:

You need to responsibly get yourself out of danger.
This is far more important to us than how many times you
binged and purged or what you're eating.

We don't need your protection and we can't let you be
free to escape by yourself. You have not gotten help.

You need a counselor who will go beyond your symptoms and talk about your sense of self and why you feel
like you're dying.

We love you but we will not sit by and watch you kill
yourself. We need for you to stay here for the summer. To
find help and remain focused on healing.

When we had prepared these words we chose to focus only
on the summer. We planned to later introduce the notion of
Andrea transferring to U.C. Davis or Berkeley to complete her
schooling. We did not want to overwhelm her with demands that
could force a swift rejection.

When Tom was through, Andrea sighed deeply and then
countered, "I can agree with much of what you've said, but I
will not stay home all summer. That is a non-negotiable for me.
I will honor my commitment to house sit."

In speaking with Jana after Andrea's death, my intuitive

feelings about Andrea's need to house sit were confirmed.[49] Andrea had called Jana and lamented about her need for some quality downtime away from her parents during the summer. Sympathetic to Andrea's need, Jana asked her parents if in her place, Andrea could watch over their home during their summer jaunts. After meeting with Andrea, the Milhons agreed that they would be delighted to help her out in this way.

I chose not to challenge Andrea's need to "honor her commitment," but I did ask, "Do Jana's parents know how ill you are?" This question was prompted by Frank's insistence that we present as if we believed Andrea was in imminent danger, even though that was not our belief.

Andrea shifted her body uneasily. My query appeared to create discomfort, but she answered simply, "No." It surprised me that she did not choose to argue with my words about the extent of her illness.

"Is that fair to them, Andrea?" I hoped that maybe this reasoning would help her change her mind, but no. Andrea rationalized that since Jana knew about her illness it was not necessary for her parents to know.

 Journal entry, November 4, 1998:

> On Halloween got dressed up as a black cat. Went to Harwood with Reena, Akila, Alana and Diedre. Was having fun until as we walked out I saw Ron holding hands with a girl dressed as a black cat—couldn't control it—I started

---

49. The original arrangement agreed to by Andrea was for her to house sit for three weeks, come home for two weeks, return to house sit for four weeks and then come home for the remainder of the summer.

to cry right then and there. We went and sat on the curb to wait for the cars. Akila and Reena hugged me. Ron came out. Walked right in front of us with arm around her. I thought I was going to shrivel and curl in on myself until there was nothing left of me. Bad weekend. I'm doing better now. This time the pain passed faster. Went to Psychiatrist. He upped my meds and put me on 5 HTP—we'll see. I'm surviving. Dad called last night just to talk. It was really nice. We've never done that before. I must be on my way up 'cuz I can't afford to go down any farther.

After many, sometimes fervent, back and forths with both Tom and me questioning the wisdom of her decision, I grasped at a desperate attempt to sway her refusal.

"Andrea." My heart pounded with emotion and my stomach tightened. I steadied my voice. "Dad and I will not hesitate to get a court order remanding your independence, if we feel you're engaging in life-threatening behavior." Tom and I had discussed this possibility earlier. I pressed on, "We are your parents. No matter your age, we are charged with the duty to protect you, even from yourself, if necessary. We will do this, Andrea." My heartbeat kept time with the repetitious mantra reverberating in my head, *Don't let her go, don't let her go, don't let her go.* I marveled at how mature and calm Andrea appeared. My statement had the potential to escalate the situation.

Instead, Andrea, with self-possessed logic, pointed out, "That is an option you have, but look at me. I am not ill. There's not a judge in this state who'd see me as a danger to myself. You couldn't even get me hospitalized if you wanted to. I am not too thin and all my blood tests are within the normal range. I am fine."

This was not the response I had hoped for. She was right. She was nineteen, an adult who had done nothing that would be legally recognized as self-endangerment. We knew our daughter's drive, her tremendous will. If we were too rigid with her, we feared she would harden beyond our reach. In hindsight, I would not worry about that for a moment. I would prefer a living, estranged daughter to a loving, dead one.

I wish I had comprehended that eating disorders kill. I certainly would have seen how deadly the situation was if we had been dealing with an illness that was a well-known killer. My response would have been one of intense concern if Andrea's doctor had said, "Your daughter has a deadly cancer. If we jump on it right now and hit it with everything we've got, there's a good chance she will heal in five to ten years. If we do nothing, or are not aggressive in our treatment, she will die." This statement is just as true if we replace the word "cancer" with "eating disorder." Sadly, those physicians who do use these more aggressive descriptors are often greeted with such intense parental denial that treatment can be compromised. And then there are physicians who, unless the patient's symptoms meet the specific behavioral criteria, do not believe treatment is necessary.[50] Following this strict protocol lets many sufferers who don't fit the "textbook description" fall through the cracks.

---

50. The behavioral criteria are outlined in the *Diagnostic & Statistical Manual of Mental Disorders-Edition Four* (DSM IV) published by the American Psychiatric Association. This is the main diagnostic reference of mental health professionals in the United States.

In her doctoral dissertation, Marcia K. Ove points out the preposterousness of this practice:

> A woman who is in her first trimester of pregnancy is not considered to be any less pregnant than a woman in her second trimester. She is expected to seek prenatal care very early in her pregnancy to avoid future problems. It would be unheard of for her to be told by her obstetrician to, "Come back when you're more pregnant." In the treatment of Hodgkin's Disease or Leukemia, waiting around for the individual to get sicker would be considered outrageous and unethical, yet it is done every day with anorexia [and bulimia].[51]

The disorder was the focus of Andrea's life. It wanted nothing less than center stage. I wish we had granted its wish and focused on nothing but her physical, emotional, mental and spiritual well-being—a challenging protocol that would have taken enormous amounts of courage. It is what I would attempt to do today.

 Journal entry, November 1998:

> Mom is right. I am using this madness, this pain as a crutch. I am going through the motions but I am not actually doing anything. I am letting myself drift farther away, become more disconnected. I am settling into this depression like a warm coat. I've lost my aura.

51. Marcia K. Ove, "The Evolution of Self-Starvation Behaviors Into the Present Day Diagnosis of Anorexia Nervosa: A Critical Literature Review" (Psy.D. diss., California School of Professional Psychology, Alliant International University, 2002), 52.

> She is right, I am on an edge. I have gotten myself here. I have allowed the situation to escalate and sweep me along until getting here—the abyss. She's right, it's bullshit and I need to stop it.
> So what is the truth of the matter? I need to get new drugs and a counselor. I need to do some laundry and some dishes and clean my room. I need to go to all my classes every week. I don't want to die. I don't want to end and I won't use insanity as a way to achieve those things because that's what I have been trying to do and enough of this fucking self-pity. My God, it's ridiculous. At a certain point even reasons are just more excuses.

After Andrea's logical response, Tom and I fell silent. Before us sat our child, a confident, gracious individual whose exterior hid, I now realize, a jumble of nervous energy, self-loathing, self-doubt, stubbornness, indignation, extreme illness and denial, but most of all, fear. I shared her fear. I was afraid to admit the reality of my daughter's illness, afraid to recognize the tremendous psychologically addictive nature of her behaviors.

Our daughter maintained the absolute appearance of a rational, thinking being. I could not accept that under the influence of her disorder, she was incapable of rational thought. I denied that Andrea could lie to us as bold-faced as she lied to herself. I knew nothing of the manipulative nature of eating disorders, or of their deceptive, chameleon-like ways.

Although the energy in our bedroom was tense, Andrea maintained a controlled exterior. I was clueless until later as to what a skillful illusion this was. I believed in the control. I thought it was real.

Mentally regrouping, I angled for a last-ditch compromise. "If you insist on returning to Southern California—and how I wish you wouldn't—then you must find a qualified therapist in the area," I urged. "It needs to be someone you can see two to three times during each of the weeks you'll be away, someone who's a specialist in eating disorders and can offer a group therapy component, as well." This was not all. I needed more if she insisted on leaving. I held my breath, and made one last requirement. "You must also agree to allow me to come visit for a week out of each of your stays." I glanced at Tom to be certain he was okay with the offering I had just made. His head was nodding agreement.

Andrea's eyebrows went up at that last request. She exhaled deeply. "I'll give you two days, Mom," her voice firm, "and I agree to find a therapist as soon as I return to Southern California. I'll interview and research until I find the right person. You have my word."

"I'll take two days," I conceded. "But a therapist must be located *prior* to your leaving."

Andrea's mouth cracked a patient smile, "That will cost a fortune in phone bills. I will find someone as soon as I get there."

That was not a prospect I wanted to even consider. "Andrea, we don't care about the costs." Knowing my next statement could anger, I borrowed from her verbiage, "This is my non-negotiable. Counseling needs to be in place before you leave this house." I knew that I was powerless to make Andrea do anything she did not choose. I was betting on our foundation of years of love and respect for her to agree.

To my tremendous relief she replied, "Okay. I can live with that." Our relief was tangible. Tom and I sighed in unison. We did not want Andrea to leave Napa, but at least she had agreed to get help. I had permission to check in on her to see her progress with my own eyes. Andrea added with sincere curiosity, "This whole thing feels so out of the blue. What prompted this dialogue?"

I responded simply, "A call from Aunt Gwenny," and I related the mostly one-sided chat in which my sister and I had engaged. The cliché "that was the beginning of the end" could be applied to the events that followed from that moment forward.

11.

Reclaim My Spirit to Nurture My Soul

There are two rules in life....
One, things never work out all the way,
And two, they always turn around.

–James Webb

When Andrea heard that it was a phone call from Gwenn that had initiated our "talk" with her, she looked stunned. She exclaimed, "You know how she exaggerates, Mom!" Tears brimmed in her eyes. "I didn't say those words to her. Believe me, I wouldn't say that to Gwenny, especially not after she informed me that if I didn't stop the bulimia, I was going to kill you."

I froze with disbelief and anger. My sister had used those words with me the night before my mother's funeral. Gwenn had not seen me during the stress-filled year of Andrea's illness and Tom's heart attack. When I walked into her home, the weight

I had lost during that time stunned her. As she hugged me she began to cry, "Andrea's going to kill you."

I pulled away. "Gwenn, Andrea did not do this to me." Glancing down at my body I looked back at her and asserted, "When I worry, I lose my appetite. It will return. It always does. This is not my daughter's fault. It is mine. This is *my* doing." I continued, now pleading, "Please, please…I beg of you, Gwenny. Do not ever say those words to my daughter. The last thing she needs right now is more guilt. If she feels responsible for my weight loss, that will kill *her*." I had extracted a promise from Gwenn that she would never utter those words to Andrea.

Amazingly, the phone rang in our bedroom at that moment. I picked up in a daze. It was Gwenn. She wanted to know if we had talked to Andrea. Weak with emotion, my voice hardly above a whisper, I greeted her with my own question. "Gwenn, did you tell my daughter the words that I begged you not to say?"

Gwenn hesitated. "Yes…but Doris, it's true. She needed to hear.…"

I can look back now and see that my sister meant only to help, but in that moment I felt incredibly betrayed. I then questioned my sister about the accuracy of all the other things she had disclosed. She suggested that Andrea had lied. While hearing my side of the discussion, Andrea began to weep softly. I could not let myself trust what my sister said. I believed my daughter. I *wanted* to believe my daughter. I desperately *needed* to believe my daughter.

Flatly, I stated, "I don't believe you."

When I hung up, I turned to face Andrea. She sobbed, "Doesn't Gwenn remember how I came and slept with her after her breast biopsy? How I drained her infected wound around the clock? How I rushed her to the hospital in the middle of the night? Doesn't she remember? How could she say I lied? How could she betray me this way?" The illness from which my daughter suffered would do or say whatever was necessary to keep itself safe. The unfortunate timing of my sister's phone call and Andrea's tears provided the ending punctuation to our conversation.

 Andrea, 19, November 1998:

> Wake Up!
> Oh my little girl
> It is time to get up now
> crawl out from under the cover of madness
> insanity is a good excuse not to live
> not to be loved
>
> Make the choice!
> step back or go over
> No loitering, not anymore
> come back to the living
> they are waiting
>
> Take back your spirit!
> your fire, your strength, your depth
> all of it
> no hiding from yourself
>
> There is a battle!

You are fighting against the world
stop fighting against yourself

You're afraid!
be honest, embrace it
scared of being wanted, loved, needed
make yourself a mess
No one can want or depend on you now
how nice
blame your misery on "them"

Go outside!
leave your haven, your safe cave
there is a day out there that wants you in it
and I think you want to be there too.

Clean up!
Do your laundry, wash your dishes
either be or don't be, stop drifting
Purgatory is Hell!

You are here
You are now
Stop sleeping today into tomorrow
there is comfort outside of your bed
Find it.
This is not an easy task
do it anyway baby girl.

After Gwenn's phone call, Andrea returned to her bedroom. We met in the kitchen an hour or so later when we both went for a glass of water. As she turned from the sink, more tears streamed down her face. My heart melted and I embraced her, the earlier mask of control completely relinquished as she wept, "Bulimia is going to take away everything I love, Mom. I don't want to lose you and Daddy." I held her away, so that I could look into her eyes. "There is nothing you can ever do to lose our love, Andrea. You will not lose us. Ever."

Later, unable to sleep, I knocked on her door. "May I come in?" I could tell by her "Yes" that tears still flowed. I walked over to her on-the-floor mattress and box springs, the bed frame relinquished during her post-Spain redecoration project. This room had provided the inspiration for the décor of her dorm room. Andrea lay under her down comforter, a favorite item she faithfully schlepped to any extended-stay destination, with one leg under, the other on top and the upper corner of the quilt pulled back to form a triangle across the bed. She often slept in this position, usually with an arm curled lazily under her head. So many parts of Andrea had changed in the past year, her obsessions with weight and diet rearranging and reordering her life and her personality. It gave me comfort and hope whenever I saw signs of the *old* Andrea.

Andrea was obviously miserable. My heart ached for the pain that I knew Tom and I had caused her during our talk. She cried, "We'll never be the way we were. Everything we talk about from now on will be this damn disorder. I want us to be able to be the friends we were, to go on walks and talk about things the way we used to. I know that can't ever be again; it's gone forever."

It is difficult for me to admit to the words I next spoke, and even more difficult to attempt to explain them. I hated to see my daughter in such agony. Growing beyond the divisiveness of our early relationship, Andrea and I had developed a deep friendship in the last few years. At that moment, I sensed she felt I had abandoned her as a friend when I tried to take back my "responsible parent" role in the conversation Tom and I had just had with her. This was a role I had almost completely deserted in the previous months. I did not realize that, in being Andrea's friend, I blinded myself to the cues I may have picked up if I had been acting full time as her parent. I identified so personally and intensely with her pain that I lost perspective. I chose, in that moment, to sacrifice responsibility for friendship.

During my childhood, truth seemed extremely subjective and situational. My alcoholic father was physically and emotionally abusive. To protect us from our father's wrath, my mother often lied. Lying became second nature to many of my siblings and me—another reason I found it so difficult to believe my sister. The integrity Tom modeled once we married helped jumpstart my progress in this area, but I reverted to my old ways in an instant when confronted with my daughter's intense pain. In my attempt to make Andrea feel that I was still her devoted friend, I lied. "It was Daddy's idea. He felt we needed to have this talk. You know how he gets sometimes."

What was I thinking? With just a few words, I betrayed our united front, our need to be actively together as parents in our concern over her behaviors. My lie had its intended effect, though. A light returned to Andrea's eyes. She looked at me and murmured, "We're still friends?"

Allowing the return of our special bond helped assuage my feelings of guilt for having just offered Tom up as the sacrificial lamb. I assured Annie that our friendship was as forever as my love for her. Andrea's relief shone across her face. Attempting to undo the one-sided concern my lie intimated, I returned to the epiphany I had during our Pitzer confrontation, "Annie, I must admit, it had never occurred to me that you might not be ready to heal. That was a shocking revelation." I needed to remind her that, I, too, had concerns, "I'd believed all along that you wanted to be free of the bulimia. In our bedroom tonight, you made it sound as if you are ready. Are you really?"

Andrea's copper pillow-flattened hair nodded, as she agreed, "I know Mom. I had that same revelation. I thought I wanted to heal, too." Andrea pulled herself into a seated position, bunching her pillow tightly between the wall and her lower back, "I didn't know until right then that I wasn't really serious—I'd just been going through the motions. On the drive home I thought about it a lot. I realized that I'm afraid to give up the bulimia, not only because I don't want to gain weight but also because it serves some purpose for me. I don't know how to explain it, but I know now that I need to get well."

The hard mass that had long ago usurped my stomach softened a bit. These were words I wanted...no...*needed* to hear from my daughter's lips, and I told her so. "You have no idea how much I needed to hear you say that, Andrea." Relief. Gratitude. Hope. Love. Emotions that allowed a chance to talk of ordinary things, like what we would do together the next day. All was right with the world again. Mother and daughter could pretend that the bulimia monster did not exist—that there was no way in hell Andrea would die in just a few weeks.

 *Journal entry, November 18, 1998:*

> I got on new medication today. Today has been good…. I'm feeling strong again. It's a beautiful thing–just like the joy in my mom's voice. I can't wait to go home–to see them and hug them and be surrounded by love to help nurture mine–I am beautiful, I am strong, I am this, I am so many things, important things. I reclaim my spirit, I take it back and I use it to nurture my own soul. Magic worked by these small hands. How much else can they do?

The next morning, it seemed as if a heavy weight had been lifted from my shoulders. Andrea's good spirits continued through our early morning walk to Starbucks. The sun beat intensely. By the time we arrived sweaty and hot at the coffee counter, our drink orders had changed from steaming mochas to two icy frappuccinos. As we left Starbucks, Andrea linked her arm into mine and proclaimed, "Today, I will not throw up at all. Not once."

Slightly dismayed I countered, "If this is truly as addictive as they say, Annie, maybe that's not such a wise promise to make. I fear it will set you up for failure. Maybe saying that you'll throw up *one* less time would be more realistic—a goal that you could truly achieve. I'd hate for you to berate yourself later if your goal isn't met. Whatdayathink?"

"Nope." Andrea was adamant. "Not once."

As I got out of bed the next morning, I basked in the sweetness of our previous day together. It was trash pick-up day, so I began my gathering rounds early. I grabbed a trash sack and headed into the study. As I emptied that room's angular, wooden container, a smile came to my lips. I flashed on Andrea's glee the evening before as she modeled for Tom her few purchases, one being the much-coveted *perfect* two-piece bathing suit. Its modest, tank top style with short trunks looked adorably sporty on Andrea. Being the first time my daughter had found a suit she really liked, I splurged and treated, spending more on a bathing suit than ever before.

I emptied the trashcan in the kitchen, then headed down the hall and entered the girls' bathroom. As I reached down for the trash I spied a large, opened, zip-lock Baggie filled with brown vomit in the sink. My stomach lurched unexpectedly. An identical closed Baggie sat in the small bathroom pail. Andrea had recently happened on this means of protecting the plumbing in her dorm room. It was the half-dozen such Baggies found in the kitchen of the Milhon's house that prompted the officers to question Jana about their meaning. Jana revealed Andrea's bulimic habits to the investigative team before their conversations with us.

Although Andrea had admitted the Baggie practice to me just weeks before, I was ill-prepared for the shock of its reality. My hand sprang away instinctively. I straightened and stumbled backwards into the hall as Andrea dashed from her bedroom with arms flailing and voice wailing, "No. No. Don't. You can't see. No, please, Mother,… no…."

Andrea spun into a thrashing anguish. I grabbed her arms. She attempted to wrench away. I held tight. Her voice became panicked, "I can't do this, Mom. I have to leave. I can't desecrate this home. I can't do what I do here. It's an abomination. I will go live with Josh in San Francisco until it's time for me to house sit."[52] With stuttered intakes of breath she choked, "I…can't…be here…and do this. I must…leave now."

Maintaining my hold on Andrea's arms, I raised my voice above her wails. "Do I find what I just saw revolting?" I cried out my own response. "Yes, Andrea. It sickens me. But that is vomit. That is not *you!*" I peered intently into my daughter's wild, frightened eyes and declared, "*You* do not sicken me. *You* do not revolt me. I love you! Nothing you *do* can ever change that. Do you hear me?" Sobbing, I continued, "What better place to be ill than in your own home, surrounded by those who love you? No, Andrea, you must not leave here. We can take this. This house can take this."

With deep moaning sobs, Andrea ceased to struggle and melted into my arms. Our bodies shook in unison, as I soothed, "Please do not think you must leave, Annie. Now, of all times, is when you must stay." I held my daughter upright and tight against my chest, massaging her limp back. Finally, her weeping subsided.

"Annie, you need to talk to someone," I whispered into her ear. "Someone skilled." I relaxed my hold a bit so I could look into her eyes. "Dad and I happened to be referred to a therapist in Texas. He's the one who helped us formulate what we said to you Friday night." Her eyes calmed as I pressed on. "He's really knowledgeable, Annie. He's willing to talk with you—it's no problem. If I give you his number, will you call him now? Please?" Purposely, I left out details as to who referred us.

---

52. Josh: a friend of Andrea's from college.

In a fragile voice, she agreed, "Okay."

We backed out of the hall into Andrea's bedroom. She sat on her café-style desk chair. I sped to get Frank Smith's number and the kitchen phone. I gave her both, and gently closed the bedroom door, leaving her alone. Knees tottering, I hurried into our bedroom. Still in bed, Tom lay on his side reading, unaware of all that had transpired. I closed our door and blurted out what had just happened. My body had difficulty remaining erect. I bent forward and propped my left foot on the edge of our waterbed's frame. My elbow rested on my knee, allowing my head, by then a heavy, pounding orb, to be cradled by my left hand, "Two large bags of vomit, Tom. That is not okay." My other hand clutched at my belly. "We spent all of yesterday together...until I went to bed at ten. She had to have binged and purged all night to create that much vomit. This is not okay. I'm scared, Tom. What should we do?"

Patiently, Tom closed his book. "You heard Frank. The number of binges and purges is not what's important. We made an agreement with her, Doris. We stick to our agreement." Tom sounded so reasonable, so sure of himself. "We give her time to do what she's promised to do. If she doesn't fulfill her part of the bargain, then we act." He admonished, "You need to calm down and give her space." I felt deserted within my own desperate fears. Again, I stuffed my gut's desire for action.

Neither Tom nor I thought of the havoc this episode played with the electrolytes in our daughter's body. Neither one of us recalled back to when I required hospitalization for re-hydration after three days of nonstop, chemotherapy-induced vomiting. We did not once, throughout the entire course of Andrea's illness, even consider electrolytes.

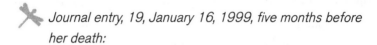 *Journal entry, 19, January 16, 1999, five months before her death:*

Winter break is over. I am back at school. It was a good break. Gary and I went to the DiRosa Preserve. We had a good time. It was a really nice date. Dad took me to the welding shop and taught me about welding. We made two froggie candleholders together.

I got my grade report today. Amazingly enough I got a B+ in Neuroscience. I'm feeling much better than I did last semester, although being down here [in Southern California] takes a lot more effort to be happy.

I was in the kitchen when Andrea returned the phone to its cradle. "I got his answering machine, Mom."

"Did you leave a message?" I sent up a hopeful, silent prayer.

"No. It didn't feel right." My heart sank.

The next day, though, I was again encouraged. Good to Andrea's word, she began her search for an eating disorder specialist in Southern California. Both she and I had read that a Cognitive-Behavioral Therapeutic (CBT) approach was often the best for those suffering with bulimia.[53] This methodology

---

53. Today, I would seek an even broader path, making sure that the therapist had experience in the Cognitive-Behavioral model but could also utilize various other approaches and philosophies as needed. Many have found specific adjuncts helpful as well, such as massage, Healing Touch Therapy, meditation, yoga, acupuncture, Tai Chi, etc. For optimal healing prospects a team approach must be considered.

purports to work on an individual's thinking patterns, while developing a repertoire of appropriate behavioral responses. Andrea spoke with a clinician at the UCLA Treatment Center. He referred her to a CBT clinic, located in the general area where she would be house sitting. It filled me with private, joyous relief when she gave me the name of the clinic. This was the same place Cynthia Rowland had recommended to me. It felt as if my prayers had been answered. On her own, Andrea found the same resource that I had held in reserve, to share only if her search came up empty handed. Andrea conducted a phone interview with a counselor there, and was impressed with her approach. She made an appointment for the day after her arrival in Southern California.

After sharing the details of her treatment search with us, Andrea asked for more information on Frank Smith, the therapist in Texas. Surprised, we gave her as much as we knew about his expertise. I mentioned that Frank had even agreed to meet with us for a few weeks at a time if we went to Texas for therapy. When I sensed Andrea's interest, I enticed, "You know, we've never been to Texas before. It could be an adventure, Annie. Counseling by day, exploration of a new place by night."[54]

"I just might do that."

Tom and I were stunned. What a coup! It seemed that the dread that had descended on my consciousness with Andrea's first phone call the year before might, at long last, be lifted. I interpreted the way that things had fallen into place and the

---

54. Another example of my inability to see the deadliness of my daughter's illness: Intensive treatment would leave no time for "sight-seeing."

shifts in Andrea's attitude as signs that everything was going to be fine. Tom and I even agreed with Andrea's request, that for her remaining ten days in Napa, there be no more talk of bulimia. We all needed a break from the illness' stressors. Besides—I believed my daughter was going to heal that summer!

 *Journal entry, January 18, 1999:*

> Today and yesterday were really nice. I have spent most of my time with Reena and Alana. We have had a really good time. I've laughed a lot.

The day before Andrea left Napa, we went for a long walk together. Towards the end of our walk, we rounded the last corner for home when I stopped suddenly with a startling return of the black cloud of unwelcome foreboding. Andrea held my hand. I turned to face her and took both her hands in mine. "You know that I love you with every fiber of my being." I looked deeply into her bright green eyes. "I'm so afraid I'm going to lose you to this." My hand reached to brush a stray lock of hair from her forehead. My eyes overflowed with tears as I flashed on a life without her. "I cannot live without you, Andrea."

This was my first reference to the disorder since we had agreed on the moratorium. Our time together, from the upheavals of the first few days to this moment, had been an absolute delight. We never saw further evidence of bingeing and purging. In fact, the bags of vomit were the only bits of proof we saw during her entire illness. Although away at college the majority of that year, when Andrea came home, we never missed food from our cupboards or refrigerator. Our alert ears never heard her vomit. After watching a recent MTV "True Life" documentary on eating disorders, I had an eye-opening realization. As with one of the young women in the special, the majority of Andrea's home binges and purges most likely happened during her frequent long drives. She took these under the guise of needing time to reflect, alone. That possibility had never before entered my mind.

Andrea tilted her head in surprise at my emotional declaration; the sunlight glinted off her thick, newly-cut curls. Her tanned body, although slender, had an athletic strength. She looked the picture of health. Matching my serious tone, she corroborated my hopes. "I know how much you love me, Mom, and *you* know how stubborn I am, how strong. Look at me. I am fine. This will not kill me. This will be one of those experiences I learn from and then help others through. I am a survivor."

 Journal entry, January 24, 1999:

Watched *Say Anything* two times. I love that movie. It makes me believe in relationships that work—they hurt but they turn out okay and people are happy.

I am too young to delve so deeply into cynicism. There is nothing wrong with a crush—I can enjoy this. It scares me, though. I'm over Ron and ready to move on and that scares me because I don't like those messy, vulnerable emotions—not one bit—and at the same time I really want someone special in my life. I feel like such a teenager— please tell me that my life does not really revolve around men! Is this because I never did it in high school?

The paradox—I have tasted desire and desire fulfilled and I want more and yet I want on the other hand to not feel or need that—to have no feelings for anyone—the repelling attraction of the ice queen persona.

I feel, too, that I haven't had long enough being over Ron—I have finally stopped thinking about him just to have my mind consumed by another boy [a young man with whom she had spent a bit of time]. I feel that I should spend time being whole and happy without thinking about any guy....

I want that thing that I see so many people have.... I don't need permanent, I don't need the love of my life—I just need a beautiful, happy, sexual relationship for a little while.... I want that experience. I want to feel like that again because it is a beautiful and affirming thing and I am so afraid that it isn't out there for me that I want to protect myself beforehand by pretending not to want it. It isn't true though. It is so very, very far from true.

I need to decide whether or not to pursue and risk hurt and play the game or to end it now and dissect him from my mind. I think that it may have to be the latter because I don't think I stand a chance. We have nothing in common—no way to get to know each other and no reason to. And unless I want to pine over him without reciprocation I think that perhaps I need to keep waiting, or am I just being a coward?

I don't know, but once again I am spending way too much time and energy thinking about boys and I think that perhaps for the sake of sanity this semester I need to make a conscious effort not to think this much over a situation I have no apparent control over.

As much as I love that movie that is not the way things happen in my life—men don't pursue me—not ones that want to stay.

My last conversation with Andrea was five days before her body was found. She phoned to chat about her new counselor. They had met two times over the two weeks Andrea had been house sitting and she felt good about their relationship.

"The therapist thinks she's found the perfect group for me. According to her, a really wonderful psychologist leads the sessions. She thinks I'll fit in well. She knows her stuff, Mom." Energetically, Andrea added, "My first group meeting is tomorrow at three o'clock. I'm excited and scared. I think it's gonna be just what I need."

"Yes!" I responded immediately. "Annie, I'm thrilled for you. Everything I've read says you need to work individually with a therapist *and* with a group to really heal."

During this last conversation with Andrea, I asked her the question I had proffered each day before. "Have you checked with your therapist about seeing her more often? Maybe three to four times a week?" I held my breath.

Fortunately Andrea chuckled, "I know, I know, you'd have me go every day if you could." She continued, "Yes, I inquired at our last session. She says I need some time between sessions to process what we discuss, and I agree completely."[55]

---

55. In an individual therapeutic setting, it is difficult to make progress with eating disordered behaviors with fewer than two to three visits per week. Again, some sort of team approach is optimum.

"But Andrea," I interjected, "at one a week you'll spend all your time just getting to know each other. This is serious. She needs to see you more often so that *real* work can begin on the disorder. More sessions can't hurt." I felt a sense of urgency that I found difficult to ignore, even though both Jocelyn and Tom had been assuring me that I was behaving in true Mom-is-over-reacting form.

Andrea reasoned, "Hey, if you count group, Mom, I'll actually be seeing someone twice a week—that's close to what you'd like!"

I made a mental note to speak directly to Andrea's therapist about this when I went down to visit her the following week. To Andrea I conceded, "You're right, hon. I need to chill out."

Changing the subject, I went on to tell her about the family I had been tutoring in English. Carlos was a student in my second grade class who had enchanted both Andrea and me. Each visit home, Andrea would help out in my classroom and spend the majority of her time chatting with Carlos. As a recent arrival from Mexico, he spoke not a word of English and was delighted and relieved to communicate with an adult who spoke his language fluently. For my tutoring, Andrea had suggested that I make game cards in English and play a sort of "Match Game" with common English phrases, illustrated with clip art.

I told Andrea I had begun playing the game not only with Carlos, but with his entire family. She and I laughed together about how Carlos' older brother, a teen who sported gang colors and had greeted me with intense suspicion, joined his mom and siblings when he witnessed the fun we had. I reported, "Carlos can't wait to see you when you come home."

Andrea's voice changed. Seriously she warned, "Don't make any commitments for me, Mom. I can't promise that I can do that."

I silently chided myself for causing the laughter to leave her voice. "Okay, hon—no expectations." I heard her sigh in relief. Changing the subject I let her know her report card had arrived. "Do you want me to open it and read the results or let it wait until you return home?"

"Oooh…no, I'd better wait till I get home. I'd rather put off knowing."

"Okey-dokey, it'll be waiting for you on your bed."

I had to ask the question that had been weighing on my mind. "Annie, did we make a mistake letting you go?"

Without hesitation, she assured me, "No, Mom, not at all. I've never been happier. It's very peaceful here, and I've had time to reflect. I needed this."

I felt relieved. "I'm so glad, Annie. I was scared that we'd made a huge error."

My daughter dutifully continued to feed me the words I needed to hear. It is only in hindsight that I recognize the charade I demanded she continue. My demands were not vocalized, they were an undercurrent of the fears and resentments and anger that I did not speak. My mouth boasted that I could handle whatever information she could give. But my body spoke otherwise, silently pleading, "Please don't tell me how bad off you are.… I really can't take it. I don't have the strength. I don't have the courage. I don't want to know how ill you're becoming. I am ashamed that *my* daughter has done this to herself." I lived blinded to the codependent behavior that came so naturally to me.

Andrea continued to mollify my guilt. "No, Mom. No mistake. Matter-of-fact, I want you to come visit for longer than the two days we talked about. You can come for a week, if you'd like." Andrea seemed to sense my jubilation at the extension of the visit limit. She gave an enticing thumbnail description. "You'll love this place. It's so adorable. There are sweet verses from the Bible stenciled on the walls in each room. The backyard is filled with gorgeous blooming flowers, many I've never seen before, and the front yard's *full* of roses. It's a gardener's paradise."

Our call ended pleasantly. Andrea reaffirmed, "I'll call tomorrow to wish Daddy a happy birthday and to tell you all about the group session…probably around six or so…."

I interjected, "Don't forget, hon, I'm taking Dad's welding night class at the college from six to ten."

"That's right. I forgot. What time would be good for me to call?"

I checked with Tom. "Dad says, 'No worries.' He's happy he got to talk to you tonight. You don't need to stress about calling him on his actual birthday."

"Well, if not tomorrow, then maybe sometime Friday or for certain on Sunday for Father's Day."

"I can't wait to hear how group goes, Annie, but we'll wait for your call."

Right before Andrea hung up, I heard the old, familiar intake of breath as her voice caught, "…Okay. I love you, Mom."

I made a conscious decision. I knew the catch in her voice

meant "ask for more," but I wanted desperately to savor our conversation. I reasoned that I would ask when she called the next day. I wanted to believe in the truth of everything she just told me, that she took her work on healing seriously, that she *wanted* to heal, that allowing her to leave home had been a good idea. I wanted my denial for just one more day. I would ask, "What's wrong?" tomorrow. Like mother, like daughter: I also wanted to put off knowing.

"I love you, too, Annie."

Andrea died in her sleep approximately six hours later. Her body was found lying in bed with one leg on top of her down comforter, the right corner pulled down in a triangle, and one arm resting under her head. She never made it home to open her report card. She had earned straight A's that semester.

12.

𝒯𝒽𝑒 𝒫𝓊𝓇𝓅𝓁𝑒 𝐵𝓊𝓃𝓃𝓎

Not until we are lost do we begin to understand ourselves.
—Henry David Thoreau

 Andrea, 19, November 1998:

Prozac Poster Child

Sip of water, wash them down
the sharp edges of the world
blur and soften
the buffer is in place

One green, one yellow, one white, one red
Love and hate them – just *take* them
and the world comes back into focus
and you can control your tears

Put the bottles back in the drawer
No one sees
and what is so terrible

about not going it alone?
Damn you Horatio Alger! I need help

Put my face on a billboard
Your sister, your daughter, your friend, your lover
I could be any of them
I bet I am
but do you know?

The good girl, the nice girl, the always "okay" girl
responsible, busy, perfect
she only cries when she's alone
tied to the apron strings of my drugs

Would you look at me like that
If I had the flu?
If I told you they were antibiotics?
If I told you your best friend takes them too?
It is dependence that is my sin
I don't stand without help
Damn me then but I choose standing.

See me!
See your brother, your husband, your child, your friend
I am all of them
work, school, play all with a smile
Poster child for all of the buzzwords you laugh about
Therapy, depression, anxiety
Bulimia, Anorexia, Prozac
What a mess!

Check your own medicine cabinet
What do you see?

Maybe what you need isn't there
Maybe you forgot it in my room.

The fragrance of cherries, Andrea's favorite fruit—that was the smell that hit my nostrils when I first entered the recently disinfected home where Andrea had died. The oily fumigation chemical, required by law, left a film of cherry essence on everything. The Milhons had the Herculean task of washing every single wall, floor, ceiling, piece of furniture, article of clothing and knick-knack, as well as replacing all their spices and pantry items after the spraying of their home. Bless them for not hating our daughter, and for showing us compassionate kindness throughout their horrendous ordeal. We could not enter the home for three days, first because it was a crime scene, and then because it was filled with bio-hazardous wastes...the emissions from my child's decomposing body. As soon as we were allowed, Tom, Jocelyn and I came to see where Andrea had spent her final days, and to gather her things to take back to Napa. Jana led us into the bedroom first.

During our initial conversation, the coroner had warned us that Andrea's bedding had to be destroyed. The mattress, the box springs, the sheets, Andrea's down comforter, all that came in contact with her fluids would be incinerated. Seeing only the metal frame of the bed, though, sent a sharp chill through my chest, cutting off my air supply for a marathon moment.

Throughout the early days of grief, conscious breathing had become a continual trial. The wind was forever being knocked, or pulled, or pushed, or blasted out of my chest. Sighs of every form, some small, some huge, some like the repeated blip on a hospital monitor screen, escaped unbidden. I had never noticed myself sighing before, but after Andrea's death, inexplicable sounds leaked from deep within my throat, my lungs, my belly. Some seemed to originate from a place as far removed as my toes. I have read that these emanations are a common part of grief. It is oddly comforting to know that others sigh, too.

I stood and stared at where my daughter had slept. Jana had promised to leave the house untouched. I needed to see how Annie had spent her final days.

I tried to take it all in. The room, as well as its corner bookcase, was filled with stuffed animals and dolls of all shapes and sizes, from Jana's youth. Andrea's one suitcase sat on the floor under the window, her backpack near the open closet. The one wall with unfinished cedar panels would need to be stripped—the cherry disinfectant had damaged the wood's fibers.

Jack Kornfield's book *A Path With Heart*, on the perils and promises of spiritual life, rested with its pages marked on the stand next to the bed, a recent gift to Annie from my sister Jackie. My heart squeezed tight when I flipped the cover and read in Jackie's flourished hand her timely inscription, "Andrea…Love yourself with an open heart."

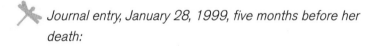

Journal entry, January 28, 1999, five months before her death:

So I'm enjoying this experience of being stable. It's a new one for me. Emotionally—I am doing damn good—I don't really know how it happened. I just know that I am reacting to things and dealing with them a little differently.

I enjoy my classes and I love that I am getting all the
reading done and really being proactive.... Things are
good—I am good.

Opposite the bed, on the desktop, intertwined within itself,
lay Andrea's silver cylindrical, locket-like necklace, a gift from
Jocelyn for her nineteenth birthday. Since receiving it, Andrea
had worn this necklace every day. It became for her a sort of
amulet. A tightly rolled scrap of paper had been coiled inside its
sterling cylindrical tube. Jocelyn had written her encouragements
for her sister in her struggle with bulimia. "Annie Lynn—I Love
You...You Can Do It!" Later, Andrea had added to this mini-pa-
per roll one of her favorite quotes from an unknown author: "And
are you going far from home? Rest assured you're not alone." She
then filled the remaining space with a message left by Tom on her
answering machine, "Hey Kid, I'm proud of you for hanging on
while times are tough. Keep treading water until you feel a current going the way you want to swim. Love you, Dad." Andrea
had recorded the date of the message, "11/9/98," seven months
before her life ended in the room in which I stood.

I raised the necklace from its resting place, allowed its twirl-
ing chain to untangle, and then draped it gently onto my neck.
Eyes clamped, I encircled the shiny cylinder with my hand,
holding it tight against my breast. When tears began to drip
from my chin, I glanced down to rescue whatever I had rained
on. I was stunned with what I saw. Hunched on the desk chair,
catching my teardrops, sat Andrea's purple bunny. Its long, too-
big aquamarine dress flowed onto the floor, as it draped over
the bunny's short legs.

The year that Andrea turned seven, my father gave me Christmas money for the girls. I needed to wrap their chosen gifts and place them under the tree at my parents' home, for the Lucas family's annual Christmas Eve unwrapping frenzy. We were so poor at the time that I delighted in the prospect of allowing my daughters to select whatever they wanted, up to twenty dollars each.

 *Journal entry, February 15, 1999:*

Joc & Tracy came down this weekend and brought Moe [their boxer]. It was a lot of fun. We saw [the movie] *Patch Adams*, visited Gwenn and went to the La Brea Tar Pits and the Santa Monica Pier and the Promenade. It was a really good visit.

During our gift selection sojourn, on our way to the down escalators in the Anaheim Mervyn's Department Store, we passed a large round table to the left of the bank of moving stairs. On this table sat a bevy of giant purple bunnies with floppy ears. The marketing ploy worked. Andrea was hooked. Her gift would be a colossal purple bunny. She and her new best friend were nearly the same height.

I figured the bunny was a fleeting infatuation. She would quickly outgrow her fondness for this furry stuffed friend and it would take up a lot of space, in our large, cardboard box home-for-forgotten-toys in the garage. I was wrong. The purple bunny traveled to Spain with Andrea, always decked out in the same, over-sized hand-me-down flowered print dress from her child-hood. By the time the purple bunny made the trek to college, its dress was worn paper-thin, the tiny flowers on the gown's transparent bodice no longer visible, threadbare from years of bedtime hugs. It would lie under the covers at her side available to be enveloped by arms as needed throughout the night. This faithful bedmate was never given a name. Andrea always called it simply "my purple bunny."

The morning after being told that everything in the bed with Andrea would be destroyed, I had awakened with the sudden, distraught question, "What about her purple bunny?"

I called the coroner frantically and implored, "Did you see a purple bunny in the bed with Andrea?" He did not remember it. Patiently, he pulled out the photos taken at the scene the day before. I begged, "Please describe to me what you see—not her body, but how she's lying…what's with her." He related, for the first time, the specifics of the position of Andrea's body: her comforter pulled back, her leg on top, one arm cradling her head. This news brought immeasurable relief.

The coroner tended to believe that choking had not killed Andrea, although he continued to investigate the cause. Up until hearing his description of the scene, images of Andrea gagging on her own vomit had tormented me. The thought that panic and fear had filled her final moments pricked at my insides like a cat's sharpened claws. I let out an enormous breath of relief when I realized that my daughter had gone peacefully, in her sleep. I knew then, before the official confirmation, that my daughter had not choked to death, and yet still…I needed to know if the purple bunny had survived.

"You're sure there's no purple bunny?" I persisted.

"There's a possibility it may have been hidden by the comforter. I'm sorry, Mrs. Smeltzer, I see no purple bunny."

Andrea had always slept with this stuffed animal. I knew she had taken it with her to house sit. Where could it be? For some reason I needed this link to her. I would not have the opportunity to see my daughter one last time, to hold her, to kiss her. I knew that her body was just the vehicle, the shell we discard when our souls leave, but I yearned for that final good-bye.

Gwenn and I had ministered over our mother's body when she died. We curled and styled her hair with the cute barrettes Gwenn had found, we adjusted her makeup—Gwenn even did her nails. I marveled at this gift...not so much for our mother. I knew she, her essence, had left this realm the day before. It was a gift for me. It allowed me to be with Mom physically one last time. Gwenn and I talked to her as if she were there. We cried and we laughed, especially at our twinge of guilt when we accidentally burned her forehead with the curling iron. It felt as if our mother laughed with us. During these hours, I began differentiating between my mom's physical form and her spiritual being. I felt cheated out of this opportunity with my own child. I wanted something. I *needed* my daughter's purple bunny!

And there it sat, slumped and forgotten, somehow spared its loving owner's fate. I grabbed this smushed purple rabbit and embraced it to my chest. I added to the wetness of the earlier tears and quietly expressed my gratitude, "Thank you, Lord...thank you, Annie...thank you." Its dress had a dark stain on the bottom hem from the fluids that had seeped from my daughter's body. This was the only spot on the bunny that did not waft of cherries; instead, it smelled of pungent humanness. It was a remnant of my daughter. I breathed in its dank rancidness and did not care.... I could hold a part of Annie.

The bunny, being almost three feet in length, had probably obscured the investigators' view of Andrea's body. It had most likely been pulled off soon after their arrival. It then blended easily into the room's ambiance. Right then, the precise scenario did not matter. I celebrated it as a miracle. As if my daughter's hand had guided the investigators to remove and then leave behind a small gift from her to me.

That moment became a vivid, lasting image of those days after Andrea's death. Four years later, on one of our annual speaking trips to the Claremont Colleges in Southern California, we visited with Jana and Victor. Jana was amazed at the amount of time that had passed—it still felt so immediate. We talked about some of our most intense memories.

Jana surprised me when she divulged her vivid recollection of my discovery of the purple bunny. Her mid-length ponytail, the color of ripe apricots, slapped at her pale eyebrows as her head shook and she explained, "When you picked it up, Doris, I remember its stink forced me to step back—it reeked of the smell of death." I listened intently as I rocked Jana's ten-week-old second son, Samuel. She went on, "I watched you clutch it to your breast with such desperation—your senses so overwhelmed, you appeared unable to smell the stench. That astounded me."

Jana's serious expression changed to baffled astonishment

when I corrected, "I smelled it, Jana. It was a part of my baby…it was what was left for me."

For Jana the horrific odor had taken her back to the trauma of finding Andrea's body—her death. For me, it spoke of my daughter's soul—her life and its continuance.

 *Journal entry, February 24, 1999:*

> [Follows a lengthy description of how Ron and his friends had suddenly reentered Andrea's life, an experience she titled "Ron Week."] I'm eating too much too late at night—to be honest, I'll probably have to throw up again—the __ time today and I just got back from my second jogging expedition. As I said, for today the score is eating disorder 1, me 0.

When we arrived back in Napa with Andrea's things after the memorial service, I began the arduous task of unpacking. Every item triggered a memory. No matter if the memories were sweet or bitterly sour, the sickening agony of putting her things away pummeled my insides without mercy. My need to rid her room of its stacks of boxes forced me to continue. Movement actually seemed to keep me alive, a self-winding watch; I created the energy to stand by the act of standing. One item would lead to a recollection that would soon engulf me with a flooding of others.

There was the yellow Pooh blanket Jocelyn had given Annie the Christmas before. At home, it lived at the foot of her bed. Gratefully, we discovered it on the couch in the Milhon's television room. It lay crumpled, as if Andrea had just risen and allowed it to fall from being wrapped around her body. Her three-tiered tackle box of serious jewelry-making supplies stood open in front of the sofa, one crimping tool left beside the blanket. Andrea had gotten an early start creating the baubles she planned to give her friends and family for Christmas.

Beside her room's light switch hung the slatted wooden jewelry holder, displaying for easy selection her eclectic earring and necklace collection, many of them painstakingly assembled by her hands. I glanced at the tackle box, now closed and latched in the corner of Andrea's room. With anguish I pleaded out loud, "I don't know how to make jewelry, Annie! What do I do with all this?" A wave of sobs wracked my frame. Everywhere in this room were reminders of Andrea's skills and creativity—the pillow she had designed, with a noble cat sitting at the edge of a Roman archway; a round full moon shining in a star-drenched sky, its embroidery needle left dangling from a golden thread. I lifted this just-begun piece and wondered anew at her ability to make the backside of her needlework identical to the front. Where had she learned that skill? Another jolt—I would never be able to ask her.

A smile nudged at my heart when my eyes caught the pair of welded dancing frog candleholders, miniature versions of one of Tom's large metal sculptures, additions to her dorm room décor completed just a few months before. I remembered her delight with Tom's lessons on cutting with a plasma torch. She had exclaimed, "It's *fun* playing with fire!"

We had placed the many boxes of Andrea's things around one of her most energetic and long-term projects, which had taken up residence on her bedroom's floor. It was to be a tri-fold privacy screen for her room at school. I stepped over the three long wood panels dividing the carpeted floor, and studied the one that she had nearly completed; it awaited only its decoupage topcoat.

Onto this panel's sea-blue painted background, Andrea had artfully placed glossy photos of animals and women from around the world, amassed from a multitude of discarded *National Geographic* magazines. She had spent the previous two years cutting, with extreme precision, the silhouettes of each body and face. Large, triangular-shaped holes topped each of the wooden screens. Andrea had made the cuts after her father showed her the rudiments of plunge cutting with a saber saw.

These three panels shouted stark reminders of all that would be no longer—not just of Andrea's physical presence, her hugs and her laughter, but of times to come. The screen's incompletion echoed the lost promise of Andrea's future…an echo embodied by the thunderous booming in my head.

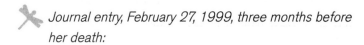 *Journal entry, February 27, 1999, three months before her death:*

Shit—I just experienced reverse peristalsis—I think.[56] I have got to stop throwing up as much as I have been—this is no good.

My stomach churned. The cherry scent covering Andrea's clothing added to the pounding in my brain and the sickening

---

56. Reverse peristalsis: the action of the muscles in the esophagus working backwards when the stomach rejects food or liquid.

of my stomach. I needed to launder her things to rid my sinuses of the offending odor. I began sorting her clothing, separating washables from dry-cleanables. With the washing machine started, I tackled her suitcase. These items had been enclosed within its zippered interior and so had, thankfully, escaped the cherry spray. Unexpectedly, I came across the bathing suit we had purchased just a few weeks before; its tags were still attached. She had not had a chance to wear it, not once…the concussive echo of things lost returned.

Holding the swimsuit, I dropped to the edge of Andrea's bed, and wailed. Like the frayed edges of a torn carpet, I unraveled. I could not handle the suit's presence in my home. If Andrea's incomplete projects spoke of unfulfilled dreams, this possession screamed of fulfilled nightmares—the need my daughter had to make herself thin enough to wear it, the method used to acquire that leanness, the media's unrelenting messages of ever-smaller sizes…my misguided camaraderie that translated to unspoken support of my daughter's weight loss when I bought the suit for her…and the cruel fact that she would never wear it. I could do no more in Andrea's room that day. When Jocelyn came home the following weekend, I insisted she take me to the mall to return the swimsuit.

 *Andrea, 19, February 1999:*

> You do not understand what they mean
> Not when they talk about heartbreak, anyway,
> not when they describe their rent open heart
> bleeding from a deep narrow puncture wound

Not when they discuss a wide hole of jagged edges
throbbing the tempo of their pain

What Drama!

Such exaggeration!

You, you know pain, intimately

You know the abandonment of your best friend,
    ditching you at your most vulnerable
You know the fear of sitting
    by your parent's hospital bed,
    a deathwatch sentry
You know the torture of Hunger,
    losing weight to "fit in" a social group or blue jeans
You know the sadness of being alone at night,
    and during the day, and around people

But you do not know heartbreak

You do not know that it is a pain
    separate from these others
You do not know that when first you feel it,
    it will take your breath away
    and knock you to the ground
You do not know that its tears are not dainty or stoic,
    they come out in wrenching torrents
    that leave your body wasted
You do not know that when asked to describe it,
    you would say that it stabs, that it cracks open
    your chest cavity and exposes you
You think that's a cliché

You do not know heartbreak

But you will
And you will learn

You will learn that the soul takes longer
   to heal than the body
You will learn it is a pain
   no one can see and you can't prove
   and you will wish it otherwise
You will learn the strangeness of a person
   whom you hate to see and long to be near
And you will learn that
   unlike any other pain you have survived,
   you would, and you will,
   Do it all over again.

And then, you know heartbreak

Nearly six months later, a surprise check arrived in the mail for close to a hundred dollars. I did not recognize the account, so it took a few minutes before I realized its purpose: the refund for the bathing suit. It arrived just days before Tom, Jocelyn, Tracy, their two dogs and I planned to escape the torment of the first Christmas since Andrea's passing, by hiding out in Carmel, a dog-friendly town.

Jocelyn advised, "Cash the check, Mom. Put the money in an envelope and bring it to Carmel. Andrea will lead us to what she'd like us to buy. It'll be like a Christmas gift from Annie."

For three days, Jocelyn and I kept our eyes open for possibilities. We both knew we would recognize the gift Andrea wanted for us when we saw it, but doubts began to form as we walked into the last shop on our final day in Carmel. It happened to be a jewelry store. I glanced into the glass case along the right wall, and there it waited.

"Jocelyn, look at this."

Jocelyn turned and peered into the case, following my pointed finger.

"Oh my Gosh. It's the gift. It's Annie's gift, Mom!"

There before us, displayed beautifully on black velvet, rested a crystalline dragonfly necklace, a duplicate of the earrings that I had purchased as a Christmas gift in honor of Andrea.

The young woman helping us gasped in astonishment when Jocelyn held it up to her neck. "Why, it matches the earrings you're wearing perfectly! Where'd you get them?"

We sang in unison, "Napa."

Still incredulous, the woman continued, "I can't believe it. This necklace isn't part of a set. It doesn't come with earrings. I've never seen them before."

We were not surprised. We pulled out the envelope labeled "Andrea's Gift" and made the purchase. The clerk noticed the envelope's title and raised her eyebrows in question. Jocelyn briefly explained that the necklace was a gift from her sister, Andrea. The clerk replied, "Well, it's a very generous gift. You'd better thank her."

Under her breath Jocelyn whispered, "I already have."

13.

The Brilliant Cleansing Truth

*The only courage that matters
is the kind that gets you from one minute to the next.*

−Mignon McLaughlin

 Andrea, 19, December 1998:

~~It is not necessarily either/or~~
Can't I be a mess and still be wonderful?
Eat and still be beautiful?
Cry and still be strong?
It seems to depend on whose eyes I am reflected in

My eyes.
How am I reflected in my eyes?
two thin lines on my wrist
a reminder of the danger in self perception

A new life
I do not look in the mirror
I do not look at the scale

I do not look for my reflection in others' eyes
I look at those two thin lines
and I wrap myself in my arms
and hold onto this gift to the world
A gift that is mine to give but not my right to destroy

Easing back into the current
a surprising fear of being swept away
This time I hold on to the shore
until I can move deliberately,
with Thought and Purpose
slow down to a crawl

I no longer hurtle into life
without brakes or cares or bumpers
I move with slow caution
like a blind grandmother
drawing her version of the world close
not to get lost in someone else's maze
tapping her path.

Deep Breath
dig ten toes into the sucking, receding sand
current flows
take my own steps
contain myself as my own separate current
not to be swept Away

I can eat, I can laugh, I can dance
I can cry, and play, and Love
I can Live
without condemnation, without reprimand

without regret
The Incredible Dichotomy of Being

It is no longer either/or
I am a plethora of ands

The summer following Andrea's death remains a fog. One thing I remember is my need to walk. It felt like a driven, relentless necessity. I needed to escape, to be somewhere else, to be some*one* else. It seemed that all I had to do was walk long enough and far enough and I could, as Andrea wrote in the opening poem of Chapter One, "belong to a different truth." In the early months, in fact years, I required exhausting physical activity. If not walking, I worked at digging holes in the yard. I planted roses in honor of Andrea, and trees, a multitude of trees. I rototilled a giant patch of ground for a vegetable garden. I dug, I planted, I walked, and not once did I manage to escape my reality of pain and grief. I tried self-medicating with cigarettes and alcohol, lots and lots of alcohol. Nothing brought reprieve. I hungered for a moment of relief…a moment, only a moment. Not even in sleep could I find release. Nightmares often shattered any wish to slumber.

I did not drive until I returned to work in late August. The concentration and focus it took to keep the car on the road proved beyond what I could muster. With Tom behind the wheel, we left Napa every weekend to be with Jocelyn and Tracy. The one-hour drive to their home always presented great difficulty. Car time allowed for the mind to go to places of intense darkness. A year later, a job-related move for them would increase our drive to their home to two hours, doubling the agony.

For the most part, I remained cloistered. If I went out in public it was in Jocelyn's town, rarely Napa. I had an immense need to avoid people we knew, or those who had not yet heard the news. When we did run into those who were unaware or were seeing us for the first time, there was the agony of reliving the experience with them in a public place.

After the tearful exchange, often necessitating our comforting them, they would continue on their way, going back to their lives. We, however, could not return to a life unchanged. These encounters left me utterly physically and emotionally drained, especially if hurtful platitudes were proffered. I often sent out a quick prayer, "Please have the courage and strength to just be with me in my pain. Do not try to minimize it or compare it to yours or others you know. I know it could always be worse. I know that my daughter is in a far better place. Please have the wisdom not to utter these words." This prayer did not often get answered, and the well-meaning attempts at comfort would rip through my chest like a jagged rock catapulted with monstrous power.

Shortly after the first anniversary of Andrea's passing, I responded to an e-mail from one of her friends. I attempted to put my experience into words. I wrote:

> This process of grief is like being tossed by waves in the ocean: Some are small swells which allow me to heave slightly upward and gently down again, others swallow me for a time, allowing quick snatches of breath before passing overhead and permitting me to bob to the surface, battered but ready for the next one.
>
> The most overwhelming and frightening are those that crash with such intensity and ferocity that my weakened

body is flung to the shore, driven deep into the sand. Chest-high, I struggle for freedom, all the while being pounded and hammered by returning waves. Any progress made is swiftly undone and drowning begins to look like an attractive option—release in one form or another is all that I desire.

Eventually the storm relents; the tide recedes and allows me to slowly squirm out of the sand. I am too exhausted to crawl further inland, and when the waters return my body is eased back out into the deep where the process begins anew. I yearn for time on shore.

The ocean seemed the perfect metaphor to describe the comings and goings in the intensity of pain, but the pain was *always* present.

During the third year, the grieving changed. I began to experience an occasional good day. I wrote the following on one such day in response to an e-mail from Kay Talbot, one of the compassionate grief therapists I had visited:

The second year of grief was darker than anything I could imagine. I felt that I was in a never-ending tunnel that tightened at times smaller than my body size. I would sit in the blackness, just running my hands along the craggy surroundings, hoping to find an opening large enough for me to fit through—frightened that I could not; afraid that I would. I rounded a corner that second summer and miraculously acquired a dim light that I now carry with me. I have made a few turns that have led me back through a bit of the tunnel I've already traversed, but the light allows me to see the jagged edges that tripped me up before, the deep crevices in which I languished. I can now see my way around and out of these hazards.

My e-mail went on to describe how I believed I had acquired the light. I mentioned the antidepressants I had taken for a number of months. I told Kay of the many articles and books I had read: one about a woman who had lost both her teenagers within months of each other; one about a man who lost his wife, mother and young child in an automobile accident. I wrote about how these had helped me see, in a new way, that my pain was not unique to me and that it could, truly, be worse.

I told of the tragic death of a new acquaintance whom I had met just since Andrea's passing. She had survived an eating disorder, earned a PhD, and worked like a champion in our attempts to educate the world on these illnesses. At eight and a half months pregnant with her first child, her heart suddenly burst from a previously undiagnosed defect. I remembered the day I learned of her death. Beyond the devastation of losing a newfound friend and fellow activist, I realized that I had no guarantee that had Andrea survived her disorder, she would not have left, prior to me, sometime later.

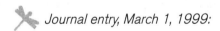 *Journal entry, March 1, 1999:*

> Just met with Jana…. [after a long description of a chat about Ron's recent odd behavior, she goes on,] I need to be careful, though. If this does mark some sort of beginning of us being friends, I need to be very careful about how invested I allow myself to become. This will be an interesting test of my convictions….
>
> [Jana] said—Why is he sniffing around, maybe he's regretting this much sooner than expected—but I don't know about that—I think if he *is* regretting dumping me

it's just 'cuz he has nothing better to do with himself at the moment.

¡Cuidado, niña! [Careful, girl!] remember that you are never going back—that you have power over your life, not him. If you remember that, then being friends will be a really nice change.

I shared with Kay the revelation I had after a fortunate session with another grief counselor. After patiently listening to me rant for over twenty minutes about how I could have saved my daughter if only I had tried harder, the wise counselor had asked, "Do you really believe you are that powerful, Doris?" She helped me see what Tom and Jocelyn had attempted to teach me for many months. At that counseling session, though, I could finally hear the words—that when we look back at the "should haves" and "if onlys" we tend to see them in a stagnant, one-dimensional realm. We forget the dynamics of the situation, the many factors involved in our decisions and in others' reactions, and how truly complicated and intricate is the reality of "then." I could not see the truth of that until the day that I felt ready.

 Journal entry, March 2, 1999:

Mom's flying in today. Grandma [my mom] is dying. She has one to three days. We're going to say good-bye.

[Mother hung on for two more months. She died on May 12, 1999—four weeks before my daughter.]

In moments of clarity like this, my mind became unburdened. For a time I could exist with my head above water. I might even have the reprieve of drifting off to sleep in this tenuous float.

The turmoil would return, however, first thing each morning. For over three years, my first conscious thought was a renewed awareness that Andrea had died. My mind could see her bingeing or I would feel the agony of her pain, her shame, my shame, her final hours. My chest would heave with the tremendous sigh that came every morning followed immediately by tears and numerous unique scenarios of how I could have saved my daughter. "If only…I should have…Why didn't I…?" Had I recorded each life-saving idea, there would now exist a treatise of over 2,191 ways to rescue someone from bulimia. When I painted my memories with the broad, blackened brush of guilt, my life appeared as a dark, opaque canvas that allowed no light, no reason, no tenderness towards self. Each day I had to begin anew, attempting to forgive myself for my humanness, experiencing success only rarely.

One day, Tom and I visited Jocelyn at work. She is the superintendent of the Folsom City Zoo Sanctuary. It is a job that suits my animal-loving daughter well. She had asked me to come speak with her grant writer and share a bit of my grant writing experience. During that visit, we witnessed our daughter being who she is as a boss. I observed her listening patiently to her employees, guiding them to make decisions on their own with gentle probes. "What do you think?" she would ask, supporting their ideas, often brainstorming solutions to problems on the spot. When others questioned something Jocelyn did, my mind was boggled at her ability to really hear what they said without taking it personally, and her willingness to modify her actions, if needed. I realized that I could easily work for my daughter. Later, I had to comment on her impressive skills.

Jocelyn listened to my reflections on her management style and then gently chided, "And where do you think I learned how to be like that, Mom?" I smiled as she answered her own question. "From you and Daddy, of course."

"Ah, but you see, Jocelyn, if I am to own that, then I must also be allowed to own the contributions I made toward the death of your sister. I can't pick and choose. If I take credit for the good, then I must also take credit for the bad."

"But I only hear you take credit for the bad, Mom. If for every time I heard you lament, 'I caused that in Andrea' I also heard you celebrate one or two *good* things you did for Annie, I'd stop getting on you about it. But I don't hear that, Mom. You only focus on the mistakes you made." Jocelyn was relentless in this area. She contended, "I was there. You raised me, too. Andrea, me, and all our friends agree, you and Daddy are the best parents ever. My friends were always so envious of my family. I wish I could convince you of that, because *that* is the truth."

Shortly after our visit to Jocelyn's place of employment, I found myself once more decrying to her my skills as a parent. After commenting for the hundredth time about how I seemed capable of only remembering the bad things I did as a mother, Jocelyn switched gears. She reminded me, "You know how you're always going on and on about the behaviors you modeled for Annie, Mom? How much they hurt her?"

"Yes." Half a dozen examples skipped through my mind.

"Well, what are you modeling for me, right now?"

Ouch. That truth hurt. I had continued the same old behaviors, just in a different venue. I demonstrated how not to forgive oneself, how to nurture guilt over past errors. Had I learned nothing from Andrea? I had wanted her to accept herself as she was, with all her flaws and shortcomings and talents, the entire "human catastrophe" even though I could not do the same for myself. Jocelyn finally awakened me to the choice I had to make: either continue to hate myself forever, or give myself what I promoted in our talks, the gifts of forgiveness and unconditional self-acceptance.

These days I work daily at seeing how I am and who I am with honesty. I practice noticing when the guilt comes, and take some time to really get to know it—to notice my response to it and its effect on me. This has seemed to lessen its power. I am flawed—which simply proves that I am human. Only God knows perfection. Accepting my multiplicity and sitting with the discomfort of my human nature, in all its shades of light and dark, has allowed my soul to grow.

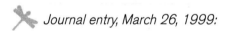 *Journal entry, March 26, 1999:*

...I am good enough. I am __ pounds, a size __. I speak Spanish and I AM A GOOD HUMAN BEING.

But the truth, the real truth is I don't believe it. I believe that I am inferior and so I gravitate towards those willing to act superior. I believe I am too large so I gravitate towards people who are, in a way hoping I'll look small by comparison.

I do not value myself in all of my wonders and contradictions and I'm hurt that [someone else] doesn't? That's backwards.... It is easy to blame [others] for my hurt but the real hurt comes from the fact that half the time I want to leave me too—that is what causes the pain 'cuz you are supposed to love yourself through everyone else's comings and goings. I need to work on healthier relation-ships—with everyone. I need to stop this strange habit of selecting friends on some supposed basis of superiority.

I'm on my way to __ pounds and I remember when I thought life would be perfect if I could just make it to __. Maybe it's time to learn how to see the perfection that's already there—after all "Being perfect means having all your parts." Not just the ones you like....

Sad though it will be if Jana's not here next year it could be a good thing—I need to redefine myself in terms of my relationships here at Pitzer. A new RA staff, a new HD, no Ron—that could be a really good recipe for next year.

I look forward to [this summer] as an experience to practice being my best self—as an experience that will shake my complacency so that I look at myself in the light of truth (as I have already begun to do) so that I can put into practice the imperative goals of liking myself, loving myself, loving my body and recognizing both my worth and my intelligence—if I don't do that how can I be any-thing but surprised when others do? And how can I ex-pect them to believe it at all if I don't live the proof? Thank you, God, it was about time for my cosmic alarm clock to start ringing the truth and knock me out of complacent self-ambivalence.

The brilliant cleansing truth of my weaknesses gives my strengths a chance to work hard and shine.

Andrea believed that everyone else had life figured out, that only she suffered from self-doubts. I think she saw the façade that she created for the world as deeply flawed when measured against the *real* confidence she assumed that others had. I cannot help but wonder, what if we all told our truths? What if our frailty was not something we felt compelled to hide? If we pretend to be who we are not, then others see our pretense as *real*. This sets us up to judge ourselves harshly against a standard that does not reflect the truth.

One of the most important goals in my life, prior to Andrea's death, was to become the best mother ever—another aspiration toward perfection. This target provided a secure hiding place for me, the me that deep down feared she had no value, could not be *good enough*, not as a mother, not as a wife, a friend, a person. I think Andrea sensed, at an almost primal level, that her mother was in hiding. Maybe if I had faced my fears, Andrea would have been able to face hers.

14.

Angel Face in Full Bloom

*The human heart feels things the eyes cannot see
And knows what the mind cannot understand.*

–Author unknown

 Andrea, 18, September 1998:

I want it to be over, don't I?
this delicious private pain I cause myself
Once so attractively seductive.
Punishment, Pain, Control, Despair
The four horsemen
stirring up my belly, flying forth from my mouth
Quema [it burns]

Their swords covered in my blood
their silent tiny wounds only I can perceive
Did they win?
Is there an enemy besides myself?

Pain, the best anesthesia

self-absorbed, thinking only of itself
Get lost in this pain, this Dolor [pain]
you created him
has he usurped his creator?

He whispers, insidious and provocative:
I am important, comforting
only me!
was there ever something more worthy to
remember?

I am a jumble, a fractured prism
reflecting, confusing, refracting
self-anesthetize
It is so easy

The seductive one
all encompassing
he taunts me, beckons me
Only in Dolor is there clarity
he erases all else
giddy–I am coming!

I can control him, my creation
all else irritates, hurts and confuses me
not him
Dolor cuts off outer feelings
floating, I cannot focus or fight

The beauty!
of condensing all confusion and chaos
into this one thing
the cunning Dolor that I can grasp

Exhilaration!
the simplicity of only one evil
one foe that is so often my friend

Dolor,
He strokes me and cuddles with me
and lets me hold him
My creation that needs my nurturance and protection
So dear to me
At once smaller and larger than me
Hide you from the world so they cannot harm you
Hide you so no one sees as you
take my power for yourself

A fascinating trap
An ingenious maze
the perfect self-constructed self-destruction
No one else can see him
and what mother could reject her own child?
wanting it to end, holding fast to what you control

Such perfection!
Such Dolor

I knew when Andrea's struggles with bulimia began that I had entered unfamiliar terrain. I thought, though, that I *knew* grief. My grandparents died and I mourned their passing. When friends lost loved ones, I generously shared with them, often in unbroken monologues, the depth of my grieving wisdom. My mother died and I began the process of mourning her death, but it was not until experiencing my daughter's passing that I came to see that I knew as little about grieving as I did about eating disorders.

I now recognize that grief does not just enter my life when those I love leave this realm. Grief happens nearly daily and its range is vast, from the pain of a misunderstood comment to the agony of watching my child suffer under the influence of a powerful illness. Not until Andrea died did I begin to recognize the years of unexpressed grief that live within me. I believe it lives within us all, and that it is this unexpressed grief that causes a tremendous amount of suffering in our lives.

Each grief, however, is experienced differently. There are those that require mere moments to be felt and expressed. Others may require years. But even that is not true for the grief I feel over Andrea's death. That grief is an ongoing, lifetime process.

The many grief counselors we visited and books we read were right: The only way out of grief is through it. To attempt to ignore or sublimate postpones the inevitable. I, like so many before me, must walk the walk. I must feel the pain and anguish and anger in order to progress within the process of grieving, a practice that will be with me as long as I live. I do not ever expect to *get over* or *recover* from my daughter's leaving. There is a spiral of phases that I continue to go through again and again, always with newly-acquired insights and knowledge.

Tom asked me the other day, "So have you reached acceptance yet?"

His question angered me. Surely *he* knew better than to think there was a stopping place, a place where you arrived and then sat forever more. I contained my anger and inquired, "What do you mean by acceptance?"

"I think I've finally accepted that Andrea is no longer here. Her death really did happen. I cannot deny it. She's not coming back."

Tom's explanation relieved me. Given that definition, my answer could be, "Yes, our daughter is no longer physically here. I have accepted that."

That often is not what is meant, though, when many well-meaning friends, colleagues, even family members ask that same question. Their meaning of "acceptance" is many times defined as a sort of closure: the place where you can finally put all of this grief behind you and get on with your life. "Just get over it," as one ex-friend advised.

This is my life. It is changed and can never be the same again. Andrea's death will always be a part of it. There are those who would like the old Doris back. She died on June 16, 1999, along with her daughter. Like her daughter, she has been reborn. Doris is in her infancy, still growing, still learning with this new awakening. She has information she did not have before. She is becoming more aware.

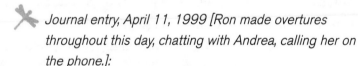 *Journal entry, April 11, 1999 [Ron made overtures throughout this day, chatting with Andrea, calling her on the phone.]:*

I'm also now in a position where I have to figure out what the hell I want—do I want to go back down that road? Is it worth it for five weeks? [Ron was graduating and would leave for graduate school out of state] Will it screw with my head if I do?

One thing I do know—I'm not putting up with the

same shit as last time. He helped create the self-confident strong woman sitting here so he's going to have to put up with her if he wants back in my life. He doesn't get to run and hide and he'd better be prepared to verbalize what he wants and talk honestly about what's going on. I don't need to drag up the past but I'm sure as hell not going to relive it, so if he wants to get something on with me he's going to have to work for it and prove that he's worth the gamble—again....

It's 1:20 and at 2:00 PM I'm going to talk to Jana to get her advice and opinion about it all.

Our culture's tendency to deny the reality of death and the multi-faceted tapestry of grief has truly crippled us when it comes to dealing with loss, either for ourselves or for those we love. We do not even have a way to identify those who may be grieving. I am reminded of an excruciatingly painful scene from the Australian movie *Rabbit-Proof Fence*. An outback officer rips three aborigine girls from their mothers' arms. As the daughters are driven away to the government home for "half breeds," the girls turn to peer out the auto's 1930s era back window. With frightened, unbelieving eyes, the youngsters witness their mothers sobbing in broken heaps on the hard dirt, and their grandmother, fallen to a seated position, repeatedly banging the side of her head with a large rock.

This grandmother's reaction resonates with my own experience. It speaks to the need to have an outward sign of inward agony. The stone to the head would give the world a bruised and bloody indicator. More importantly, it would give the individual proof positive of the anguish inside. It seems to me that those whose grief is immense would benefit greatly if we returned to some means of indication, some outward symbol, such as the black armband of old, without restrictive time limits or expectations about its removal. Such an emblem could serve to formally externalize our pain. Upon seeing it, we would know to tread lightly, to ask about the one who had died and to respond by *listening* with empathetic compassion. This, along with the realization that we are all somewhere along the grieving continuum, seems a far kinder approach.

Instead, our culture continues to rely on the teachings the early psychologists ingrained in our psyches. We trusted their wisdom. They saw mourning as a process with a beginning and an end.[57] Since the time of Freud, it has been theorized that grief is resolved and closure achieved, once emotional detachment is attained. For me, there has been no detachment or closure. What I do have is integration, the ability to live my life with the full knowledge and acceptance of the fact that my daughter died. For me, this integration includes the fact that Andrea is as much a part of my life now as when she was physically in this realm with me, sometimes even more so. Fortunately, there are wise theorists who validate my own experience and who see an ongoing emotional attachment to a dead loved one as a sign of health.[58]

Kay Talbot, who in addition to counseling others through grief is an accomplished researcher and author, reminds us in her book *What Forever Means After the Death of a Child*, that "healing

57. Jane E. Coles, "Enduring Bonds: Sibling Loss in Early Adulthood" (Psy.D. diss., Massachusetts School of Professional Psychology, 1996), 4, 27.
58. Ibid., 27.

evolves—it is not a destination."[59] When reading Kay's research, I found great comfort in the fact that she had limited her subjects to those with five years or more of bereavement because it appears to take many parents at least that long to move beyond acute grief when a child dies.[60] There are those who started giving us "get over it" messages in our second and third years. To that type of behavior, Kay responds, "It is vitally important to remember...that there is no one way to survive the death of a child, no proven method of processing grief that ensures the best possible accommodation to this traumatic loss." Her next statement hangs on a wall in my office. "It is our society's unrealistic expectations that parents should 'accept' and 'get over' their child's death that frequently causes secondary injury and anguish to many bereaved parents."[61]

Countless authors on the subject mention the twisted reality that "grief rewrites your address book." Friends dear to us for many, many years are no longer close. Grief must be shared. We must be allowed to howl our pain again and again in the presence of others. Some of our dearest friends, by their response to our howls, made it very clear that we must take that need elsewhere. And we have.

Andrea introduced me to the person who has become my most steadfast partner in grief, miraculously, after she died. I had not finished reading all of Andrea's journals while in the Southern California hotel room before her first memorial service. About a week later, I grabbed one of her notebooks as I crawled

---

59. Kay Talbot, *What Forever Means After the Death of a Child* (New York: Brunner-Routledge, 2002), 211.
60. Ibid., 23.
61. Ibid., 3.

into bed and resumed reading where I had left off. The page was dated June 3, 1997:

 Andrea, 17, one week before high school graduation:

There are so many things I will miss about this room next year. I love sitting here in the twilight, incense burning, fan blowing, rain drizzling outside. It is peaceful and happy and makes me feel restless yet content. This room has turned into such a part of me, it is my sliver of Spain here in America. It is the physical expression of that content joyful feeling I had in la tienda [a reference to the deli owned by her second Spanish family] of watching the tormenta [storm] out the window. It is beautiful and melancholy and a dorm will never compare.

Next year excites me. I feel interested and alive as high school has never made me feel. At the same instant—I have finally been able to enjoy my childhood for two years and I suppose I wish I had more time to experience it with my new outlook. Quite a dilemma....

These philosophical contemplations are probably due in part to the Water World tragedy.[62] Although I did not know very many [of the students involved] and at that, not well—There is a certain camaraderie between seniors who have only seven days to go.

One dead and 32 wounded. Those things aren't sup-

---

62. Water World tragedy: One of the slides collapsed at this Concord, California amusement park, plunging its riders into a drop of "30 to 40 feet [onto] mud, dirt, concrete, rocks, flowers, bushes and each other." Source: U.S. Consumer Product Safety Division Report, Washington, D.C., 20207, December 31, 1997, *http://www.cpsc.gov/library/foia/foia98/idi/34d214d.pdf*.

posed to happen seven days before graduation. My heart breaks for Quimby—17 and ready to go out and conquer life—death is so cold and infinite....

So tonight I will pray for innocence lost. I will pray for the healing which follows heartbreak, and I will strive to hold on to this moment...so that this death is remembered and so that, in a small way it is not in vain.

From heaven I pray that [Quimby] will influence more of us than perhaps she ever could have in life. This is the best I think any of us can strive to do now for her. It is perhaps the most sense that can be made of it. Her fall did not kill us—at least it can make us strong.

The knight does not go flying out under a fanfare of triumphant notes resplendent in shiny metal. That armor has been dented and the knight is left to wander dazedly saying—that COULD HAVE BEEN ME!!! Seven days till the rest of our lives and it could have been any one of us....

I weep for the graves of us all—not just Quimby's but for the end of childhood—of carefree innocence—Yes, this is the last summer, especially now. The last summer of this room of looking out the window with my 17-year-old eyes. This is a beginning—partly horrific and partly beautiful. It is a beginning of the real world, of a place without parents who can always kiss it and make it better. It is a quirky place and this will not be the last death we will experience, but it will perhaps remain in the memories of our souls long after other wounds are healed. It is at once a distant tragedy without direct filial effect and one of the most deeply felt experiences many of us will have for a while.

I know that one day…it will seem long past but I write this now so I won't ever allow myself to forget the lesson. Life is precious, it is over faster than we can blink, we are never invincible. Truth is not eternal and human memory is as short as human life.… I want to have this ingrained on my soul so that I remember that all of my life's moments are important and worth my full, wholehearted partaking. Even the Cuenca moments, because seven days before graduation we lost one of our own and our shiny new armor was given an indelible mark.

I cried as I read portions of this journal entry out loud to Tom. It amazed us at the impact Quimby's passing had on Andrea. They attended rival high schools in Napa, yet Andrea felt a deep connection to this fellow senior whom she had never met. "Quimby's mom needs to read this, Tom." I reached behind me and turned out the light over our bed. "I know I would want to know if Andrea had affected someone this deeply."

"You're right. Do you know how to get hold of her?"

I settled under the covers. "I think my friend Carol Mongelli may know. I'll give her a call tomorrow and see if she can get the number for me."

I was awakened the next morning by our phone's loud jangle. "Doris, I'm sorry. Did I wake you?" It was Carol.

"Not a problem. I needed to get up." I contained a yawn as I marveled, "I planned on calling you today."

"I'm so sorry for waking you…but I felt led to do this. I don't know if this is right or not…" Carol hesitated and then her careful words came rapidly. "I think it's important for you to connect with Quimby's mom. I've called to give you her number."

The synchronicity of this phone call amazed us both. I call it another miracle.

I phoned Victoria later that evening to ask if we could meet sometime in the next week or two. With kindness, she promptly offered, "I can be there in fifteen minutes, if tonight works."

Meeting Victoria felt like commiserating with a fraternal soul. Victoria knew my feelings. Even in her great sorrow, a mere two years since her only child's passing, she could sit with me in my pain. With an anguished need to know, I kept asking, "How? How did you survive? How are you still alive?"

I remember Victoria gently rubbing the sides of my folded hands, which dwarfed hers, a reflection of her petite stature. Over the next few years I would come to know this woman's strength and forbearance, and realize that there was nothing small about Victoria's courage, her heart or her will. Thick, golden ginger hair caressed her neck as she shook her head and responded with sincere honesty, "I don't know. Somehow you do."

I wanted her to tell me it got better, easier. I wanted to hear that the pain would stop.

With complete openness, her intense blue eyes looked straight into mine. "It gets different."

Watching Victoria survive has made me believe in my own ability to survive. At eight years out, she is actually beginning to thrive. I know that our daughters brought us together.

One year after we met, Victoria had a life-changing experience when she saw the medium John Edward in San Francisco.

In a room with about two hundred others, John spoke to Victoria about Quimby. He gave her so many specific names and dates that Victoria had no doubt that her daughter had visited through John. This brought tremendous comfort to my friend—indeed, she celebrates it as her faith-day. Prior to John Edward's reading, Victoria believed dead meant "no longer." She did not believe in an afterlife or in the continuance of the soul. She knew that I had a strong faith in God, but wanted Tom and me to experience some of the same healing in which she took such immense joy. Through events that are miraculous in their own right, and not mine to tell, we ended up visiting John Edward at a taping of his television program at his studio in New York.

John is a fast-talking, muscular young man from New York. His youthful looks and no-nonsense demeanor shatter many stereotypes about mediums. The day we met, he wore a casual, long-sleeved, blue crewneck sweater atop his signature jeans. He stood on stage, hands intermittently forming triangles with the meeting of his thumbs and fingers as he began with an explanation.

"One thing I like to do is remind people that you don't need a medium to make a connection with the other side. It's an ability you can work to develop within yourself."

This certainly matched my own experience.

Victoria, Tom and I sat in the farthest corner of John's studio gallery, stage left. I watched with fascination as John shared messages with various audience members. It appeared his accuracy was remarkable. John had begun wrapping up the long day when he suddenly pointed directly at me and stated,

"I think I'm here…older female who wants to be known.… I'm getting Mom, your mom has passed?"

The surprise of being called on so late in the day caused my mind to go blank. My hesitations and screwball answers seemed to frustrate John. There were things he said that were point-blank accurate, and then other things that made no sense to me. Midway through he asked, "Do you understand why they show me that the birth month and the death month might be the same?"

I tried to think quickly, but I had mush for brains. I guessed, "My mother died a month before my daughter?" John paused and glanced downward in concentration, considering my response.

Victoria offered, "My mother died the same month as my daughter."

John nodded, "That's what I'm looking for—the two things that are the same—I thought it was a celebration, though." He stopped himself and then said, "No, they're telling me it's the birth month…hold on—just give me a second—for one of you the birthday is also the same month."

I jumped in with a sudden realization, "Oh! My mother and daughter were both born on the twenty-ninth!"

"That's what I'm looking for—the same dates."

John rapidly moved on, and we thought no more of this interchange until over three months later when I awoke with an "ah-hah." I rolled over in bed and awakened Tom with a question. "When did Andrea die?"

Tom answered groggily without opening his eyes. "June 16. Why?"

Ignoring his question, I pressed on. "And when is your birthday?"

"June 16. You woke me up to be sure I knew those dates??"

I explained my sudden revelation to Tom—all of us had completely forgotten that the anniversary of Andrea's death is the same month and day as Tom's birth. While in New York, we suffered from what John Edward calls "psychic amnesia."

At one point during our reading, John puzzled, "Who's Dulci, Dulcinea?" Those are not common names and yet they are what Andrea called her beloved pet ferret.

John directed a question to Tom. "Who's Jim?"

"We have a friend named Jim." Tom responded.

"I'm telling you that somebody from over there is acknowledging Jim in a big way...either he eulogized her or he did something to speak about her and she's telling me to thank him." John smiled broadly, so did Tom. At this point, I held my hand under my nose to attempt to halt the flow of tears.

Although I have continually felt touched by Andrea since her passing, having John Edward validate her presence by offering specific facts did seem a remarkable blessing.

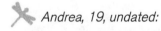 *Andrea, 19, undated:*

> Something smells like home tonight
> A little bit like love
> I don't suppose it's you though.
> I don't suppose it could be
>
> I hardly ever think of you anymore

Hardly ever at breakfast and hardly
Ever at lunch
Hardly ever all night long

There is a hunter in the sky
We are all in his sights
But it is we who choose our punishment
And we who mete it out

Ceramic still life
Like the picture I hold of you
Unchanged since parting ways
The image I may hold of you forever
And it is already wrong and outdated
As must be your image of me

Strange lies we tell ourselves
I have never not been in my bed alone
How can it feel lonely?
You never had a place there
But that is where I miss you

A squished banana feeling between my ears
Thick, gooey and impenetrable,
goes well with peanut butter
I wonder if we ever sit and wonder
About each other wondering about the other
Simultaneous thought is so intimate when two
People are together
And so distant when you're not

It was Andrea's twenty-first birthday, October 29, 2000,
sixteen months after her death. I looked out our family room

window and noticed that one of our five tree roses, the exquisite lavender Angel Face, stood in full bloom. That late in the fall the other rose bushes were filled with rounded rosehips and spent leaves. But not Angel Face, a gift the year before from two friends in honor of what would have been Andrea's twentieth birthday.

After breathing in the sweet perfume of Andrea's anniversary roses, my bare feet took me to the end of our patio's walkway. I threw my arms skyward and scanned the expansive sea of blue with tear-filled eyes. I embraced myself in a symbolic hug and whispered, "Happy birthday, Annie."

Still in my summer pajamas, I turned to get out of the cold. I stopped and my heart skipped. There, tucked into the backside of Angel Face in the midst of the plethora of purple, quite unexpectedly, grew one perfect white rose. In that instant, it felt as if I could hear Andrea's voice exclaim, "Hi Mom!"

Straightaway I sent an e-mail to my two friends, again thanking them for their generosity, and wrote of Andrea's greeting through the unique appearance of the white rose. I told them that their gift truly "kept on giving."

Later that evening, one of Angel Face's benefactors knocked on our front door. "I need to see the white rose," she said to Tom and me.

Out on the patio, my friend gazed in amazement. She encouraged, "Have you counted the blossoms?"

That had not occurred to me. We began...one, two, three... "Oh, only twenty."

Tom reminded, "Did you count the white one?"

We had not—twenty-one roses on Andrea's twenty-first birthday.

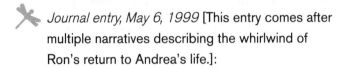 *Journal entry, May 6, 1999* [This entry comes after multiple narratives describing the whirlwind of Ron's return to Andrea's life.]:

> For such an intense and painful year the end has been pretty good. I like hanging out with Jana, Ashley, Sue, Nancy and all of them. I'm with Ron, I'm the thinnest I've ever been, I'll have a relaxing summer, there are a lot of really great things in my life, things and social interactions that I don't want to end.
>
> How ironic that I spent most of a year missing Ron and looking forward to his leaving and never having to see him again and now I will miss him and don't want him to leave.
>
> [By the following week, Ron had dumped Andrea for the final time. This was her last journal entry—she died four weeks later.]

It was midway into the torturous second year of grieving, the time without the numbing effects of denial that made it far worse than the first year, that Andrea gave me another comforting sign. I woke crying on a workday at about four thirty in the morning. I did not want to awaken Tom, and so quietly crawled out of bed and tiptoed into Andrea's room. Sitting on the edge of her bed in the quiet darkness, I rocked back and forth clutching her purple bunny to my chest as I sobbed into its soft, matted face.

I begged, "Please, Annie. I need a sign—something to tell me you're all right. Please, baby…anything." I begged God to allow my daughter to send me a message. I cried and I begged and I rocked. By the time I needed to dress for work, it felt as if I had already lived the day. Exhausted from my tears and pleadings, I returned to my bedroom. I leaned against the doorframe for a moment, with head and shoulder propping me upright.

Tom opened his eyes. He could see my state. He greeted me tenderly. "Mornin', hon."

Before I could reply, the light in our bedroom slowly came on and then went off just as slowly. It did it again. Tom mused, "What're you doing with the light?"

I pushed away from the entry and showed him my hands. "I'm not touching the light."

Again and again, the light above our heads gradually brightened and then dimmed back into darkness. I smiled, closed my eyes and spoke directly to our daughter. "Thank you, Annie."

Tom puzzled, "How do you know it's Andrea?"

"I just spent the last few hours in her room, begging for a sign. She's telling us she's okay, Tom." It seemed that she made sure to make her sign last a good long time, so that I would have no doubt that this message came from her, and was something more than an electrical snafu.

15.

Read Under and Between Lines

And are you going far from home?
Rest assured you're not alone.

—Author unknown

 Andrea, 19, written after a visit to the Sequoia National Forest, November 1998:

Earth song
Heart song
My song
Nature's endless basin
Outstretched beneath my swinging feet

Fill the chest, expand the lungs
Life, rushing in and out on the breeze
Up here I am endless,
Up here I am strong
Somehow

Standing next to this Great Sequoia
I am mighty
These trees do not dwarf me with their majestic power
They teach me of my own

Towering up, massive red stalk
Largest Living Thing on Earth
Deep forces coiled within
It fights back when struck

You see the ferocious limbs
Whipping back at the wind
Resolute in the freeze
And yet…

With the right breeze,
The right moisture
And a slurping sucking burp!
Pulled out of the Earth
Crashing and splintering
Force turned against self

All that Power, Strength and Size
With roots too small and shallow
To support it in its fury

I am small
I am near the ground
I am soft
I do not have mass to protect me

Some days I bow and stoop
My forehead trailing the ground

Some days I bend and fall
But I am not uprooted

My roots are small but wiry
Thin but deep
Spreading out in a weave through the earth
Deep tendrils into the molten core

I stand with my cheek
Pressed against the cold bark
Listening...and I hear

And I know that I am as strong as this tree
Even more resilient
Than this Giant

Great Sequoia
Largest Living Thing
And me.

About a year ago, I made a desperate visit to a therapist friend of mine. She listened with gentle patience as I filleted my insides. I thought my motivation to speak with her came because of concerns I had at the time for Jocelyn. My friend knew otherwise, but chose to allow me to express my surface pains.

With great emotion I exclaimed, "I see my daughter using food to fill a hole inside herself that has nothing to do with her body's need for nourishment. It seems that she eats ravenously to quench an emotional thirst that will never be satisfied with food."

Michelle wondered, "Is this adversely affecting her life? Do you think her health is at risk?"

No, those were not my worries. I could not articulate the fear

I felt inside—it sure seemed to be connected with Jocelyn. I spoke. "Well, what I see is not an eating disorder per se, but it is disordered eating." Tears dampened my cheeks. At that time, I still felt I owned the lion's share of the responsibility around Andrea's illness. Had I created another disorder? I wondered...had I done it again? I whimpered out loud, "Two for two, Michelle. That's one hundred percent. What kind of mother creates disordered eating in both her children?"

There seemed to be a moment of hesitation from my friend. Maybe she struggled between choosing to confront me with what I could not see at the time and empathizing with my words. When she spoke, I knew that her thoughts had not been verbalized before, and yet she saw my need to hear. So she courageously commiserated. "I have four children, Doris...." Michelle's tight, ebony ringlets bounced with her head's movements as she bravely went on to chronicle each of her daughters' and son's relationships with food and eating. Although not one of her children suffered from an eating-disorder-with-capital-letters, each one illustrated a step or two away from a balanced relationship with food—no different from Jocelyn, no different from me.

"You see, Doris, you are not alone. I am four for four—one hundred percent." Michelle looked into my eyes intently and repeated a fact that becomes truer with each passing year. "It is difficult to find anyone in our culture who is *not* in some way a disordered eater."[63]

---

63. A notion that may explain why so many of us do not take eating disorders seriously: In Western culture we are surrounded by the symptoms, yet they are often ignored, or even encouraged, despite their deadliness and the need for intensive and extensive treatment.

With that said, I could be moved toward a more honest appraisal of my real concerns. Upon reflection, I realized that the worry I claimed to have for Jocelyn was merely a projection of my own insecurities and discomforts. My narcissism and denial were showing. I had been, once more, unable to own the uncomfortable feelings within me around *my* body, *my* eating and my guilt around Andrea's death. Jocelyn was actually doing fine. It was I who was not.

Michelle looked skyward for a moment and then described an image she had of me. "I see you, in my mind's eye, digging holes." Her reference to one of my earlier pastimes surprised me. "You go here and dig a while, and then there. You dig and you dig and you dig, attempting to find the kernel...that *something* that will explain how you caused Andrea's death. You exclaim, 'Ah-ha, maybe *this* is it.' And then later, 'Oh, *this* must be it.'" Michelle smiled slowly. "You cannot find it, Doris, because I do not believe it exists. There is no one thing you did wrong. It seems that the idea you hold to—and correct me if I'm wrong—is that if you had been a *good enough* mother Andrea would not have died. True?"

I nodded, fresh tears blooming as Michelle continued, "Do you see the cycle you've put yourself in, Doris? The only way you can see that you were a 'good enough mother,'" her hands indicated the quotation marks, "would be if Andrea were still living. She is not living. So no matter what evidence you find, it will never be enough."

My tears were flowing as Michelle directed, "You need to forgive yourself, Doris. I want you to please forgive yourself."

I remember choking through sobs, "I thought I had."

With care Michelle replied, "You may have...but it's time to do it again."

Yes, time to do it again. Why was I surprised by the need for repetition? Even now, I tend to think that once I have "been there, done that" I will never need to "be there and do that" again. It was time for me to forgive myself. And a few weeks later, it was time again. I imagine that in the years to come, there will be many more times.

It was after Jocelyn turned thirty that I had an important revelation—in hindsight it appears so simple and self-evident. My daughter is an adult on her own journey. I was not the supreme influence in her life, just as I was not the only influence in Andrea's life. Not everything that happened to my children, or every choice they made, was a direct result of my parenting or me. I would never burden my own parents with such responsibility, nor would I want them to see me as merely an extension of themselves. The paradox is that although our journeys *are* intertwined and full of intersections, each is unique and on its own path. When the path is simultaneous, we must share and not attempt to commandeer the road.

Codependence, enabling, narcissism, denial—my prior-to-Andrea's-death self felt little resonance with these descriptors. Now, through my habitual patterns of living I see the influences of generations of familial alcoholism, depression, drug use, various compulsions and excesses. I look around at my colleagues and friends and see this same humanness reflected back at me. It seems that it is this state of being human, this multiplicity of imperfection and beauty that connects us. I am not alone. I hold one piece of the puzzle. If we each secret away our piece, then we, as a community, are doomed to forever search for a wholeness that can only come when we offer our pieces to each other.

At the end of one of our recent "Andrea's Voice" presentations, Tom attempted to express the importance of community and sharing feelings. He began by stating, "It has been said, 'Men think, women feel.'" The emotions that are ever-present during our talks surfaced as Tom took a few deep breaths before he continued. "Well, losing Andrea has taught me how important it is to express emotions and feelings—indeed, as people, we need to share to connect. It is through community that we can heal."

Tom's index finger reflexively pressed against his upper lip as he regained composure. With tears welling in his eyes, he glanced in my direction and declared, "Doris and I are here with you because we have been transformed in how we think about food, weight and relationships." His voice deepened and cracked. "It took our daughter's death to initiate that transformation."

Tom paused, and then added a crucial realization. "Eating disorders are *powerful* teachers."

There have been many powerful teachers in my life—people, places, experiences. They appear to be provided by God, as they are needed. My illusions of control are being replaced by an expanding consciousness...and yet...the mysteries continue.... The joy *is* in the journey.

Andrea, 19, January 1999:

So few of my writings are happy
A worrisome discovery
If someday these were the only remaining
accounts of me
What picture do they paint?

Bleak and Midwinter Gray

Though I know this life to be good,
Happiness and joy are no strangers,
That is not reflected on the white lines of immortality
Which hold my blood and tears

When there is Pain, when there is Madness,
Then there is Inspiration to dissect and ponder.
When life is good no questing need be done.
"Happy" is depth enough,
Living replaces Analyzing

Only the moments of anguish,
Hurt, confusion, and anger
Are trapped by my pen,
Moments of searching,
Desperately seeking order and happiness in words,
Explanations and Hypotheses,
Epiphanies.

Troubling,
BUT—the joy is in there.
Between questions, between lines
A story of learning and awareness of life

A fluid story,
A half told story and not entirely mine.

Stories of the Journey
Contain infinite joy,
A joy that pierces and burns and pains.

Stories of the Destination
Contain only peace.
But these stories are rarely told
There is no need, all is understood, the quest is done
Those are not my stories.

Look carefully
Judge kindly
Read under and between lines
The Journey is never so clear as the Destination
And the telling is more confusing still.

Epilogue

This book had its beginnings shortly after the second anniversary of Andrea's death. I finished the first draft on June 16, 2004. It seemed appropriate that it be completed on the fifth anniversary of her passing.

In the past two years, I returned to graduate school fulltime and reduced my work time to fifty percent. During the 2005/2006 school year, I volunteered as a Marriage and Family Therapist Trainee to gain the fieldwork hours needed to complete my degree in Counseling Psychology. Our "Andrea's Voice" presentations continue. We recently established the non-profit Andrea's Voice Foundation to provide educational outreach on disordered eating and related issues. Jocelyn gave birth to our first grandchild on Easter Sunday, March 27, 2005. So many *opportunities for learning*, as Andrea would say.

One of these opportunities recently arose in my graduate program. It was there that I first met Sobonfu Somé. Sobonfu teaches Westerners about the indigenous wisdom, rituals and initiations of her people, the Dagara tribe in West Africa. In her tradition, individuals with serious illness are given high regard. This status comes because of the understanding that these people hold something the village has ignored. The villagers know they must look deeply into their community and speak about that which is not being voiced, or more will become ill.

Andrea held, for our family, the things we could not bring ourselves to hear or to see. What if she, and all those who have died or suffer with an eating disorder, hold such "unspeakables" for the community in which they live—or for the entire culture? What are the things we are not willing to discuss? What behaviors are normalized so that profits, not personal well-being, can be attained? How many must become ill before we are willing to look?

Acknowledgments

It takes a village. This familiar cliché feels trite and sappy. Yet, when I think of it in terms of the writing of this book, it is transformed into an elegant statement of truth. It communicates my experience precisely. On our website, *Andreas Voice.org*, there is a "Special Thanks" page. The ways that I felt supported and held throughout the time since Andrea's passing had to be acknowledged and celebrated. The process of writing this book is no different. Thanks must be given.

The synchronicities of how people and experiences have come into my life continue to amaze and astound me. I tend to think of them as miracles, but by whatever name, they are phenomenal events for which I am truly grateful. I thank God for providing them.

Dr. Tesa Carlsen, my remarkable therapist, who read the very first completed draft of these pages, has given encouragement, suggestions and belief in the power of what I was attempting to do. It is this talented and gifted professional who, through the numerous resources she provided, led to my meeting the extraordinary author and editor, Hal Zina Bennett. Hal has buttressed my confidence, guided my rewrites and lightened my spirits with his wit. (Me: "As the sun rose outside...." Hal: "Where *else* would it rise?") Hal's ability to ask simple, straightforward questions that spark one's imagination is a rare gift—his tremendous creativity is evident in each chapter title. He "got" what I was attempting to do. He knew that this book went beyond *memoir*—he helped me, with his profound intuition, to focus my message so that others could hear it.

Hal introduced me to Jan Allegretti, a compassionate, intuitive editor who excels in the areas of grammar where he would rather not tread. Jan's gentle guidance has gone way beyond the mechanics of writing. In a soulful way, she came to know Andrea and me and our vision of a world unfettered with body woes. Her suggestions on utilizing quotes from Andrea in unique future formats as well as to publish a collection of Andrea's poems, brought not only a smile to my daughter's face I'm sure, but a clear direction for my next projects. Although we have never met face-to-face, it feels as if I have been working with a long-time friend.

Victoria Nelson, a dear friend, who has held my hand throughout and has generously given me hours of her life to listen, encourage, support and gently nudge. We are kindred spirits, soul sisters. Words of gratitude do not touch the love and thanks I feel for her.

Patricia Whitt, another dear friend and hiking buddy—who has given me support and valuable "hill" time. She, too, has listened with an open heart. She has gone way out of her way to get my manuscript into the hands of those who see the timeliness and power of its message. I trust her. I bless her.

Family members who have provided support in incalculable ways, especially my sisters and sisters-in-law: Jackie Lucas, Betty Lucas, Sharon Amato, Gwenn Lucas, Rose Lucas, Deborah Smeltzer, Diane Cherni, and Denise Smeltzer; my brothers and brothers-in-law: Richard Lucas, Charles Lucas, Bob Lucas, Don Lucas, Wally Gresl, Steve Golub, Dave Smeltzer, Bob Smeltzer, David Kingsbury, and Matt Cherni. A special mention must be made of the ongoing financial support for Andrea's Voice and tremendous efforts of my sister and brother-in-law, Deborah Smeltzer and David Kingsbury in bringing our Foundation to non-profit status just in time for the book's publication.

Tom's folks, D.L. and Ginny Smeltzer, my parents, Paul and Marie Lucas, my grandparents and all the other ancestors and guides from the other side who have provided inspiration and succor for my soul during some of my darkest and most needy moments. Andrea's *hermano de España,* Sergio de Isidro Hontana who, without knowing it, forced me to begin the process. Lindsey Hall Cohn at Gürze Books, for her initial encouragement, Leigh Cohn at Gürze for saying "Yes" and Lindsay Woolman at Gürze for supervising the entire project and for her many hours of editing. I had heard horror stories from other authors of how they'd been completely left out of the decision-making process on every detail of their book's layout and appearance. Not so with Gürze. Lindsay Woolman very kindly included me in her decisions and listened to my suggestions. She responded promptly to every question I had while at the same time treating me with compassion and respect. Carolyn Costin for convincing Gürze to look again. Margie and Kent Williams for taking time out of their full lives to offer publishing words of wisdom, and Clio, the Muse of writing, who joined all these others to guide me through the reorganization of chapters and several rewrites.

My friends Caitlin McCain and her partner, Katie McGonigal, for valuable input on my original book proposal. Sarah Chennault and her niece, Emma Davis, who sat with the first three chapters *ad nauseum* and helped me formulate my early thoughts. My other lifetime friends: Meg Scrofani, who has become a mentor as well as friend; Alice Cornwall, who not only helped arrange for Andrea's transition-home in Spain, but has given me much support; Carol Mongelli and Karen Connolly who, without knowing it, contributed greatly to my survival. These two women gave up hours of their valuable time to meet with me every other week for nearly four years. The influence of their friendship was recently confirmed when I ran across research that had been done on the power of relationships. The study I read dealt with terminal breast cancer patients, but its outcomes fit with my experience. Its five-year-follow-up illustrated the power of community—only the women in the support groups survived; Jim Elder and Karen Kiefer, true-blue friends who have been in our lives since Tom and I first met—if not for the daily breakfasts Jimmy provided in the early months, I know that the first meal of those days would have been the dinners prepared by others.

Michelle Minero, another friend and fine therapist who thoughtfully reflected my "hits" so that I could forgive my "misses." Vicki Cameron, co-author of the important book, *If Your Adolescent Has an Eating Disorder*, who listened with sensitivity, made suggestions and really cared. Liz Blumberg at Mass Bay, for sharing Jane Coles' doctoral dissertation so that I could better understand Jocelyn's experience of losing a sibling in early adulthood. Marcia Ove, for allowing me to delve into her dissertation, and Melissa Walters at Boudoin College for her willingness to help and for adding her support to my hunch that the book needed to be different than the talk.

The Institute of Imaginal Studies for providing a rich learning environment that helped initiate me into deeper consciousness. Cohort 11 friends and companions from the Institute—my transformative learning buddies—who have provided me with many lessons: Carren Potter, the very best roommate with whom one could ever hope to share the graduate student experience, who has listened, read, walked, and listened some more. During the middle of a very busy workday, this dear friend took the time to brainstorm headlines and book description rewrites. She saved my addled mind. Dan Lee, who has never failed to show genuine interest in my journey, especially my writing—his monthly query, "How's the book?" became a musical refrain for my sometimes-weary heart. And all the rest: Sivi, Don, Steven, Janine, Kier, Renjitham, Jessica, Rochelle, Kayleen, Mary, Ursula, Fred, Stephen, Terry, Dianna, Cheryl, Mark, Lianne (for her right-on marketing ideas), Jen, Stuart, Chris, and especially Keiko O'Leary.

Keiko, with textbooks to read and papers to write, kindly offered to peruse the manuscript with her talented editor's eyes.

She wanted to help make this book "the very best it could be." There are re-writes that I know she felt would have vastly improved this volume, but it was time for me to stop—striving for perfection would have supported the very attitude that helped kill my daughter. This text is as imperfect as I. Thanks to Keiko's judicious help, it is far better than it would have been.

To all of those extremely busy professionals who graciously read the manuscript and wrote heartfelt endorsements I send my sincere thanks: Hal Zina Bennett, Frances Berg, Douglas Bunnell, Jeanine Cogan, Kate Dillon, Dean Edell, Emme, Margo Maine, Abigail Natenshon, Carol Normandi, Laurelee Roark, and Ira Sacker. Carolyn Costin, for graciously volunteering to write the Foreword. Erik Stangvik for seeing the importance in my message and for reminding me that there are two sides to every story. Sharon Newport, the dynamic and talented co-producer of the documentary film, *America the Beautiful,* for kindheartedly offering to schlep the manuscript to others for possible endorsement, and to Rob Johnson, a gifted graphic designer, for creating a book cover that took my breath away when I first saw it.

Jocelyn Smeltzer, my daughter, who has read and reread this book nearly as many times as I. Wise beyond her years, she has provided essential signposts directing me in tone, content, grammar, punctuation and style. Her life is busy and full, and yet she has generously given time no matter how inopportune. My son-in-law, Tracy Work, who in the first weeks read my initial attempts and pointed out, "Tom's a big guy, Doris, but you give me no sense of his size, his looks, his presence. I need to see who you're talking about." This critique, along with his many other right-on suggestions, caused me to examine every book thereafter with an eye toward the author's craft. I became a student of the word. Jocelyn and Tracy's newly born son, Fischer Lynn Work, who brings with him the promise of tomorrow, and has provided me with the opportunity of becoming a student of grandparenthood.

My husband, Tom, who has steadfastly held the vision, especially during the times when my sight became myopic or blurred—he is my companion, my lover, my best friend, my mirror, my prodder, my support—the one whose presence forces me to look where I would rather not peer.

Andrea. I saved her for last. I had hoped that the words to express my gratitude to her would percolate to the surface of my mind by the time I made it this far. *Pero, no hay palabras... corazón...no hay palabras. ¿Entiendes, mi hija? ¡Mil gracias! Con mucho cariño.* I miss you beyond words.

Appendix

Possible Characteristics, Warning Signs and Risk Factors of Eating Disorders

Characteristics

- Extreme sensitivity and vulnerability
- Taking care of others before self
- Low self-esteem with feelings of inadequacy
- Black and white thinking: good/bad, dangerous/safe, all/nothing
- Difficulty expressing emotions and feelings
- Poor coping with life events
- Body dissatisfaction
- Depression, anxiety, anger or loneliness
- Perfectionism, driven, achievement-oriented
- Obsessive/compulsive behavior

Warning Signs

- Dieting (promotes binge eating)

- Frequent weight fluctuations (or a marked increase or decrease in weight not related to a medical condition)
- Calorie counting
- Bloating/nausea/abdominal pain
- Compulsive or excessive physical activity
- Constipation
- Frequent meal skipping
- Substance use
- Restrictive eating pattern or abnormal eating habits: preference for strange foods, withdrawn or ritualized behavior at mealtime
- Early sexual activity
- Guilt after eating; secret eating or bingeing
- Recent withdrawal from friends or feelings of isolation, depression or irritability
- Unrealistic weight goals or an intense preoccupation with weight and body image
- Lack of period or irregular periods
- Thinness as a valued goal
- Thinning hair

Risk Factors

- Dieting (promotes binge eating)
- Cultural focus on a "thin ideal"
- Traumatic, abusive experience (sexual or otherwise)
- Narrow definitions of beauty
- Genetics
- History of being teased based on size, weight or physical appearance
- An experience causing a sudden weight loss (wisdom

teeth extraction, hospitalization, etc.) that is then reinforced by continual comments and compliments

- Cultural norms that value people on the basis of physical appearance and not inner qualities and strengths
- Family history of obesity or eating disorder
- Parent(s) with:

  chaotic lifestyles

  high achievement expectations

  alcoholism/substance abuse

  driven, perfectionistic styles

  ongoing weight/fitness focus

  depression

Compiled from various sources:
National Eating Disorder Association (NEDA) 1-800-931-2237, *www.nationaleatingdisorders.org*, Seth Ammerman, M.D., and the Something Fishy Website, *www.somethingfishy.org.*

Eating Disorder Resources

This is not an exhaustive list of resources—it provides a place to begin the search.

Important Books

Many of the books listed are available through the *Gürze Eating Disorders Resource Catalogue*. Call for a free catalogue (800) 756-7533, or see their website at *www.bulimia.com.*

Albers, Susan, *Eating Mindfully: How to End Mindless Eating and Enjoy a Balanced Relationship With Food* (Oakland: New Harbinger Publications, Inc., 2003).

Bacon, Linda, PhD, *Eat Well: An Activist's Guide to Improving Your Health and Transforming the Planet* (San Francisco: Linda Bacon, 2006). Available through *www.lulu.com/LindaBacon*.

Baker, Catherine, *FED UP: College Students & Eating Problems* (Carlsbad: Gürze Books, 2003).

Berg, Frances, *Children and Teens Afraid to Eat: Helping Youth in Today's Weight-Obsessed World* (Hettinger: Healthy Weight Publishing Network, 2001). Available through *www.healthyweight.net*.

Chödrön, Pema, *When Things Fall Apart* (Boston: Shambhala Publications, Inc., 1997). American-born Tibetan Buddhist nun—teaches meditative practices. A good start: *Good Medicine* audiotape or CD available through Sounds True, (800) 333-9185 or *www.soundstrue.com*.

Collins, Laura, *Eating With Your Anorexic: How My Child Recovered Through Family-Based Treatment and Yours Can Too* (New York: McGraw Hill Co., Inc., 2005).

Costin, Carolyn, *The Eating Disorder Source Book: A Comprehensive Guide to the Causes, Treatment and Prevention of Eating Disorders* (New York: McGraw Hill Co., Inc., 1999).

Fodor, Viola, *Desperately Seeking Self: An Inner Guidebook for People with Eating Problems* (Carlsbad: Gürze Books, 1997).

Fraser, L., *Losing It: America's Obsession with Weight and the Industry that Feeds on It* (New York: Dutton, 1998).

Friedman, Sandra, *When Girls Feel Fat: Helping Girls Through Adolescence* (Toronto: Harper Collins, 1997).

Gaesser, Glenn, PhD, *Big Fat Lies: The Truth about Your Weight and Your Health*, Updated Edition (Carlsbad: Gürze Books, 2002).

Goodman, Laura J., and Mona Villapiano, *Eating Disorders: The Journey to Recovery Workbook* (Philadelphia: Brunner-Routledge, 2001).

Hall, Lindsey, and Leigh Cohn, *Bulimia: A Guide to Recovery* (Carlsbad: Gürze Books, 1999).

Herrin, Marcia, *Nutrition Counseling in the Treatment of Eating Disorders* (New York: Brunner-Routledge, 2003).

Herrin, Marcia, and Nancy Matsumoto, *A Parent's Guide to Childhood Eating Disorders* (New York: Henry Holt & Co., 2002).

Johnston, Anita, PhD, *Eating in the Light of the Moon: How Women Can Transform Their Relationships with Food* (Carlsbad: Gürze Books, 2000).

Koenig, Karen R. *The Rules of Normal Eating: A Commonsense Approach for Dieters, Overeaters, Undereaters, Emotional Eaters and Everyone in Between!* (Carlsbad: Gürze Books, 2005).

Lesser, Elizabeth, *The New American Spirituality: A Seeker's Guide* (New York: Random House, 1999).

Lock, James, and Daniel Le Grange, *Help Your Teenager Beat an Eating Disorder* (New York: Guilford Press, 2005).

Lock, James, Daniel Le Grange, Stewart Agras, and Christopher Dare, *Treatment Manual for Anorexia Nervosa* (New York: Guilford Press, 2001).

Maine, Margo, PhD, *Father Hunger: Fathers, Daughters, and the Pursuit of Thinness* (Carlsbad: Gürze Books, 2004).

Maisel, Richard, David Epston and Ali Borden, *Biting the Hand that Starves You: Inspiring Resistance to Anorexia/Bulimia* (New York: W. W. Norton & Company, 2004). Contains vital information for caregivers but most important are its chapters for parents and loved ones on how to become an "Anti-Anorexic/Bulimic Ally."

Natenshon, Abigail H., *When Your Child Has an Eating Disorder: A Step-by-Step Workbook for Parents and Other Caregivers* (San Francisco: Jossey-Bass, Inc., 1999).

Newman, Lesléa, *Somebody to Love* (Chicago: Third Side Press, 1991). Out of print.

Normandi, Carol, and Laurelee Roark, *It's Not About Food* (New York: Putnam, 1998).

Normandi, Carol, and Laurelee Roark, *Over It: A Teen's Guide to Getting Beyond Obsessions with Food and Weight* (Novato: New World Library, 2001).

Pipher, Mary, PhD, *Hunger Pains* (New York: Ballantine Books, 1995).

Pipher, Mary, PhD, *Reviving Ophelia* (New York: Ballantine Books, 1994).

Roth, Geneen, *Breaking Free From Compulsive Overeating* (New York: Plume Books, 1984).

Roth, Geneen, *When Food Is Love: Exploring the Relationship Between Eating and Intimacy* (New York: Penguin Books, 1992).

Sacker, Ira M., MD, and Marc A. Zimmer, PhD, *Dying to Be Thin* (New York: Warner Books, 1987).

Satter, Ellyn, *How to Get Your Kid to Eat...But Not Too Much* (Boulder: Bull Publishing Company, 1987).

Satter, Ellyn, *Secrets of Feeding a Healthy Family* (Madison: Kelcy Press, 1999).

Tribole, Evelyn, and Elyse Resch, *Intuitive Eating* (New York: St. Martin's Press, 2003).

Walsh, B. Timothy, MD, and Vicki L. Cameron, *If Your Adolescent Has an Eating Disorder* (Oxford: Oxford University Press, 2005). A must-have book for parents—how I wish it had been available to me. I disagree with their views on "overweight" and dieting, but otherwise this is an up-to-date, incredibly valuable resource.

Wann, Marilyn, *Fat!So? Because You Don't Have to Apologize for Your Size* (Berkeley: Ten Speed Press, 1998).

Weiner, Jessica, *A Very Hungry Girl: How I Filled Up on Life...And How You Can, Too* (Carlsbad: Hay House, 2003).

Wolf, Naomi, *The Beauty Myth* (New York: William Morrow & Co., 1991).

Activism

Eating Disorders Coalition for Research Policy and Action
www.eatingdisorderscoalition.org
An advocacy group formed to advance the federal recognition of eating disorders as a public health priority.

For Families

The Body Positive
www.thebodypositive.org
Teaches young people to creatively transform the conditions in their lives that create their body image and relationship to food.

Dads and Daughters
www.dadsanddaughters.org
Provides media alerts as well as tools for men to be better fathers and advocates for their daughters.

Daughters

www.daughters.com

A newsletter/magazine for parents of girls.

Empowered Parents

www.empoweredparents.com

Extensive family information from Abigail H. Natenshon, author of *When Your Child Has an Eating Disorder: A Step-by-Step Workbook for Parents and Other Caregivers.*

New Moon Magazine

www.newmoon.org

An ad-free magazine edited by and for girls ages 8-14.

Women Express, Inc.

www.teenvoices.com/issue_current/weabout.html

Publishes *Teen Voices* the magazine by, for and about teenage and young adult women, fifteen and up.

Organizations & Information

Academy for Eating Disorders (AED)

www.aedweb.org

For eating disorder professionals; promotes effective treatment, develops prevention initiatives, stimulates research, sponsors international conferences and regional workshops.

Alliance for Eating Disorder Awareness

www.eatingdisorderinfo.org

Educational information including hotline phone numbers, treatment centers, and referrals for treatment and valuable recommended reading.

Andrea's Voice [The author's website]
www.andreasvoice.org
An informative, essential website for eating disordered sufferers, friends and parents.

Anorexia Nervosa and Associated Disorders (ANAD)
www.anad.org
(847) 831-3438
Provides help for those struggling with an eating disorder.

Anorexia Nervosa and Related Eating Disorders, Inc. (ANRED)
www.anred.com
An informational site.

Eating Disorders Association—United Kingdom and Beyond
www.edauk.com/other_organisations.htm#euro
To find resources in Australia, Asia and Europe.

Eating Disorder Referral and Information Center
www.edreferral.com
For referrals to eating disorder specialists, treatment facilities and support groups. Also information on getting insurance coverage for treatment and more.

Eating Disorders Information Network
www.edin-ga.org
Atlanta-based resource and referral resource. Quarterly magazine, speaker's bureau, curricula, school outreach programs, EDAW events.

EDA Eating Disorders Anonymous
www.eatingdisordersanonymous.org
A "balance, not abstinence" 12-step fellowship. Free literature.

Family and Friends Against Disordered Eating (FADE)
www.fade-on.ca
Excellent resource. Although FADE is located in Canada, this website is an easy-to-maneuver wealth of information.

FREED Foundation
www.freedfoundation.org
Offers some funding for eating disorder treatment.

HEED Foundation (Helping End Eating Disorders):
www.heedfoundation.org
(516) 694-1054
Provides eating disorder education, professional referrals, programs consisting of support groups, education series, annual conference, and services such as speaking engagements and community outreach.

Massachusetts Eating Disorders Association, Inc. (MEDA)
www.medainc.org
(617) 558-1881
Newsletter, referral network, local support groups, eductional seminars and trainings, speaker series.

National Eating Disorders Association (NEDA)
www.nationaleatingdisorders.org
(800) 931-2237
A valuable resource for referrals and information.

National Eating Disorders Screening Program (NEDSP)
www.mentalhealthscreening.org
(781) 239-0071
Eating disorders screening, education, and outreach programs.

Remedy Find
www.remedyfind.com/hc-eating-disorders.asp
A free, international and unbiased site that allows individuals to
rate the effectiveness of various treatments.

Something Fishy
www.something-fishy.org/
Eating disorders information and connections.

Voices Not Bodies
www.voicesnotbodies.org
An all-volunteer organization dedicated to eating disorders awareness and prevention education. Endorsed by ANAD. Holds an
annual candlelight vigil in Washington, DC.

Treatment Centers and Programs

All Eating Disorders Require Professional Help

For a comprehensive listing, please see the *Gürze Eating Disorders Resource
Catalogue* or visit *www.gurze.com* for links to numerous facilities.

Related Resources

Health At Every Size (HAES)
A size-acceptance philosophy supported by the following:

Abundance: Resources for Transformation of Body, Mind & Spirit
members.aol.com/abundancebooks
Recommended books, videos, organizations, websites, etc., for
personal transformation and healing. Contains a section on size
acceptance and eating disorders/body image.

Body Positive
www.bodypositive.com
Boosting body image at any weight.

CurvOlution
www.CurvOlution.com
A live-performance-art celebration of the female body. Beauty is not a size!

Fat-Acceptance Diabetes Support List
users.telerama.com/~moose/fa-diab.html
For fat-accepting diabetics and hypoglycemics who wish to get control of their disease. No "trying to lose weight" talk allowed.

Health At Every Size Journal
www.gurze.com
Previously known as the *Healthy Weight Journal*, this publication offers research, theory and practice supporting the HAES movement.

Healthy Weight Network
www.healthyweight.net
Authoritative research on dieting, the failure of weight loss programs, eating disorders, obesity, overweight, size acceptance, diet quackery, and HAES.

Hugs for Better Health
www.hugs.com
An alternative to dieting program. Located in Canada.

Largely Positive
www.largelypositive.com
Teaches that weight is not a measure of self-worth. Gives tips on how to improve self-image and self-esteem, even if occupying a larger body.

Largesse
www.eskimo.com/~largesse/
Network for Size Esteem, an international clearinghouse for information on size diversity empowerment.

Media Literacy and Media Activism:

About-Face
www.about-face.org
Body image and the media...a forum for letting advertisers know how you feel about their ads.

Center for Media Literacy
www.medialit.org/
A nonprofit educational organization dedicated to promoting and supporting media literacy education.

Common Sense Media
www.commonsensemedia.org
A family-friendly entertainment guide.

Media Education Foundation
www.mediaed.org/
A nonprofit organization devoted to media research and the production of resources to aid educators and others in fostering analytical media literacy. Makers of the excellent video, *Slim Hopes*.

Media Literacy
www.medialiteracy.net
Media literacy for prevention, critical thinking, self-esteem.

We Insist on Natural Shapes (WINS)
www.winsnews.org

(800) 600-9467
Dedicated to education and media advocacy. Curricula for elementary through high school.

Pediatrics

"Children and Adolescents With Eating Disorders: The State of the Art" (January 2003)
Article on the care of children with eating disorders.
www.pediatrics.org/cgi/content/full/111/1/e98

Pediatrician's Policy Statement for Identifying and Treating Eating Disorders (January 2003)
www.aap.org/policy/020003.html

Self-Help

Beyond Hunger
www.beyondhunger.org/
Offers freedom from the obsession with food and weight.

The Body Positive
www.thebodypositive.org/
Teaches young people to creatively transform the conditions in their lives that create their body image and relationship to food.

Eating Disorders Anonymous (EDA)
www.eatingdisordersanonymous.org
Contact: 18233 N. 16th Way, Phoenix, AZ 85022
A "balance, not abstinence" 12-step fellowship. Free literature.

Food Addicts in Recovery Anonymous
www.foodaddicts.org
A 12-step, self-help fellowship. No dues or fees.

Grant Me the Serenity Self-Help and Recovery
www.open-mind.org
Descriptions and access to a multitude of eating disorder websites.

Heart of Healing
www.heartofhealing.net
A site devoted to Healing Touch, an energy based therapeutic approach to self-healing.

OA Overeaters Anonymous Headquarters
www.oa.org
(505) 891-2664
A 12-step, self-help fellowship. Free local meetings.

Self-Injury

Healthy Place
www.healthyplace.com/communities/self_injury/healingtouch/facts.htm
An online community for people seeking support, info, or friendship. Has transcripts from online conferences.

S.A.F.E. Alternatives
www.safe-alternatives.com/
(800) 366-8288
This is a treatment program, but it does have a toll-free number to call for more information.

Size Acceptance

Amplestuff
www.amplestuff.com
Everything for big people, except clothes.

Council on Size & Weight Discrimination, Inc.
www.cswd.org
(845) 679-1209
Advocates for plus-size people. Provides education and information in fairness in employment, medical treatment and media images.

Fat Acceptance
www.cat-and-dragon.com/stef/fat.html
For a list of Fat-Friendly Health Professionals in states throughout the U.S.

National Association to Advance Fat Acceptance
www.naafa.org
Advocacy, education and support for heavy people, and a great book store.

Size Wise
www.sizewise.com
Information and resources for a healthier, more comfortable and more complete life.

Grief Resources

This is not an exhaustive list of resources—it provides a place to begin the search.

The Compassionate Friends (TCF)
www.compassionatefriends.org
National office:
P.O. Box 3696
Oak Brook, IL 60522-3696
(630) 990-0010
Toll-Free: (877) 969-0010
An international organization providing support and comfort for
bereaved families.

To honor the memories of our children:
TCF Worldwide Candle Lighting® Ceremony
This event is held every year on the second Sunday in December
at 7:00 p.m. for one hour local time around the globe—a 24-hour
wave of light in memory of all children who have died.

For those touched by suicide:
The Gift of Keith
www.thegiftofkeith.org

American Association of Suicidology
www.suicidology.org

American Foundation for Suicide Prevention
www.afsp.org

On-Line Grief Support
www.GriefNet.org
An Internet community of persons dealing with grief, death and
major loss.
www.KidSaid.com/
The companion site to *GriefNet*, provides an environment for kids
and their parents to find information and ask questions.

Grief-Resource Books:

Bernstein, Arlene, *Growing Season: Life Lessons from the Garden* (San Francisco: Wildcat Canyon Press, 2004).

Ericsson, Stephanie, *Companion Through the Darkness: Inner Dialogues on Grief* (New York: Harper Collins, 1993).

Jenkins, Bill, *What to Do When the Police Leave: A Guide to the First Days of Traumatic Loss* (Northfield: WBJ Press, 2001).

McCracken, Anne, and Mary Semel, *A Broken Heart Still Beats: After Your Child Dies* (Center City: Hazelden, 1998).

Sittser, Gerald L., *A Grace Disguised: How the Soul Grows Through Loss* (Grand Rapids: Zondervan Publishing House, 1995).

Somé, Sobonfu. *Falling Out of Grace: Meditations on Loss, Healing and Wisdom.* (El Sobrante: North Bay Books, 2003).

Talbot, Kay, Ph.D., *What Forever Means After the Death of a Child: Transcending the Trauma, Living with the Loss* (New York: Brunner-Routledge, 2002). A publication of research findings and their application in the lives of those whose children have died.

About the Authors

(10-29-79 to 6-16-99)

Andrea Lynn Smeltzer, 19, was trained in opera, enjoyed the theater, was an avid dancer and masterful at making jewelry and crafting poetry. After studying in Spain for a year at the age of fourteen, she spoke Spanish fluently. At the time of her death she was studying German, with a plan to master Japanese next. Prior to college, Andrea was elected president of her high school's Amnesty International group and was an outspoken advocate for human rights: She was the representative chosen to present the student petitions to the Guatemalan consulate in San Francisco in 1996. At Pitzer College she was awarded the prestigious Fletcher Jones Scholarship, worked as a Resident Assistant and Mentor, majored in International Business and Politics—and looked forward to saving the world. She died tragically after thirteen months of bulimic behaviors on June 16, 1999.

Doris Smeltzer, an educator for nearly twenty years, was thrust into the world of eating disorders through Andrea, her nineteen-year-old daughter, who died of bulimia. Doris and her husband, Tom, have keynoted at numerous conferences and presented at universities and organizations internationally. As the first bereaved parents invited to present before a congressional briefing on eating disorders in Washington, D.C., their story has now been told in the headlines of periodicals and in radio and television spots from New York to California. Their website, *Andreas Voice.org*, averages over a thousand hits a day from twenty-nine countries—testimony to the vast expanse of these deadly illnesses. Doris was named Napa County's "Community Hero" in 2003, received her Masters Degree in Counseling Psychology in May 2006 and is the co-founder of the nonprofit organization Andrea's Voice Foundation which is dedicated to education and support for everyone touched by eating disorders. When not educating on disordered eating and providing training on bully prevention and character education, she is happy to garden and work on projects with Tom in their Northern California home, which they share with their cats and llamas. Doris especially enjoys spending time with her daughter Jocelyn and son-in-law, Tracy, and dancing with her grandson, Fischer Lynn.

Contact Information:

Andrea's Voice Foundation
P.O. Box 2423
Napa, CA 94558

www.AndreasVoice.org
doris@andreasvoice.org

Order at www.gurze.com
or by phone (800) 756-7533

Andrea's Voice...Silenced by Bulimia is available at bookstores and libraries and may be ordered directly from the Gürze Books website, *www.gurze.com*, or by phone (800) 756-7533.

FREE Catalogue
The *Eating Disorders Resource Catalogue* features books on eating and weight-related topics, including body image, size acceptance, self-esteem and more. It also includes listings of nonprofit associations and treatment facilities and is handed out by therapists, educators, and other health care professionals around the world.

Eating Disorders Today
This compassionate and supportive newsletter for individuals in recovery and their loved ones combines helpful facts and self-help advice from experts in the field of eating disorders. Quarterly subscriptions available. Request a sample issue.

www.gurze.com
Visit this website for additional resources, including many free articles, hundreds of books, and links to organizations, treatment facilities and other websites.

Gürze Books has specialized in eating disorders publications and education since 1980.